W9-BCX-367

DEC 1977

RECEIVED
OHIO DOMINICAN
COLLEGE LIBRARY
COLUMBUS, OHIO

1911 OHIO DOMINICAN COLLEGE

LIBRARY

1216 SUNBURY RD.
COLUMBUS, OHIO

JOHN MASEFIELD

JOHN MASEFIELD

A CRITICAL STUDY

BY

W. H. HAMILTON

KENNIKAT PRESS
Port Washington, N. Y./London

821.91
M396H
1969

JOHN MASEFIELD

First published 1922
Reissued in 1969 by Kennikat Press
Library of Congress Catalog Card No: 70-86022
SBN 8046-0613-7

Manufactured by Taylor Publishing Company   Dallas, Texas

TO

MY WIFE

103308

For generous permission to include the quotations from his various books I have to thank Mr. Masefield himself; and also the publishers, Messrs. Elkin Mathews, Grant Richards, William Heinemann, Sidgwick and Jackson, Williams and Norgate, and J. M. Dent & Sons, Limited, who have graciously confirmed this.

W. H. H.

CONTENTS

JOHN MASEFIELD

I

INTRODUCTORY

THE humblest · reader—the veriest freshman—must feel himself in this Georgian day like a king : even that most glorious king before whom the pie was opened and the birds began to sing. April, it would seem, has come again to England ; on every orchard bough the chaffinch sings, and there is much singing of each song twice over by wise and other thrushes. Yet as recently as a dozen years ago it was possible for a venerable archdeacon preaching in a college chapel to cast a shadow of despair over a host of young poets' hearts by declaring with assurance that since the death of Tennyson Apollo had tied up his golden scroll (presumably for ever) ; and on every hand this tragic croaking was accepted as a truism with no great lamentation. Indeed, except in Ireland—where the poet could walk with his head in the air and make the claim of Seanchan in *The King's Threshold*—it was common for the writer of verse to be regarded as decidedly eccentric. Not that the age was orthodox—far from that— but it did not break out at *that* point. It may have dismissed Sir William Watson and John Davidson as minors, without reading much of their work—it was slightly interested (motive and manner alike that of indolence) in the ditties of religious scepticism or denial. It had been told, and believed, that Stephen Phillips was the coming man. It had heard amusing anecdotes of Mr. W. B. Yeats's alleged abstraction, and decided that the poetry of an Irishman who saw green elephants following his neighbours couldn't have anything to tell it. It had hardly heard of A. E. Housman, and possibly even its archdeacons had never heard tell of Robert Bridges. " *Bridges to Kipling ?* " quoth a prominent citizen, entering my study and lifting an anthology, " I shouldn't have thought Kipling required any bridges to him. Meaning's quite simple, eh ? " But *he* may have been the gentleman who asked " What are Keats ? "

Nobody makes such mistakes to-day. The Georgian renascence is an unmistakable phenomenon. Where recently it was not possible to name a single living poet, almost anybody now can point to a score. Broadsheets, chapbooks, anthologies, group-schools, volumes, collected editions are the order of the day ; poetry societies flourish ; poetry reviews and bookshops appear and thrive ; and the rarer critic is not awanting ; iconoclasm has more abundant life—" Ring out the old ! "

No doubt there is something excessive about it all ; so much new wine has gone a little to the new age's head, and inspired a somewhat comely truculence towards the great and placid Victorian age and all its works. The Victorians, however, can take good care of themselves ; the sturdier Georgians generously condescend to admit that Tennyson, with all his flaws, remains. One sometimes feels that surely something is due also to the few unfortunates who must be called mere Edwardians but who—in a thankless and quite extraordinarily barren decade— kept the lamp alight and stood scornful of scorn for Beauty in a blatant and vulgar day. They are, however, a small company. Most of them had begun to write before the great Queen died, or have lived to raise their voices still amid the Georgian band ; and among these latter we must count Mr. John Masefield.

Enthusiasm has occasionally prompted his admirers to regard him as one of the sources of the singular revival ; but it is passing doubtful if any such claim could be upheld. It is a kindlier, if more modest, estimate of his work that regards it as one of the earliest fountains to overflow the native source and become a river making glad the cities of man. What and where the source is is harder to say. Contemporaries are apt to be a little bewildered by an outburst of song and to be extravagant of praise or unduly suspicious and conventional—but some of us are sure that there is a great underived originality from which the music is drawn. At the same time there are few of the new poets whose verses bear no traces of Mr. Yeats's influence—even Mr. Walter de la Mare's beautiful *Arabia* seems to whisper of *The Happy Townland* and other fairy poetry of that master's—and everywhere, everywhere ring echoes of that glorious and unique book of lyrics, Professor A. E. Housman's *Shropshire Lad*, which was perhaps the first definite open revolt against Victorian conventions in verse and thought, although Mr. Hardy's then unpublished poetry must share the distinction. Mr. Yeats himself, and Mr. Kipling with him, were not altogether untinged by the *fin-de-siècleisme* and Yellow-Bookery of their own early days, and although that is a trace of an earlier revolt against Victorianism, it also is sufficient to identify them slightly with the age and art now revolted from anew; but Mr. Kipling for a little while, and Mr. Yeats perhaps to this day, has had an influence that may have been germinal and vital to the new art. Nor must the work of a far greater poet be overlooked. Robert Bridges is in the Victorian age, but not of it. His work refuses to be classified. It is not for an age. Its sheer beauty of rhythm, rapture and restraint alike has permeated silently, or nearly so, the mind and heart and song of every poet alive, and the Georgians unanimously and enthusiastically acclaim him their king; but he may be much more than their king. His songs have something of his own creative power and life, and they will not be a spent force in our time.

That that abomination of desolation, the Great War, has had much to do with the great wave of new poetry we may at least take leave to doubt. Whether the emotions and passion of the period, with its ravening chauvinism and its splendours of renunciation, have given a voice to the mute smouldering revolt against all Victorian and neo-Victorian conventions in verse and poetic thought, or whether the same upheaval of feeling only won a new opportunity and more tolerant and eager listeners for the poets—probably always a majority of our youth— cannot be confidently decided, of course. There is much to indicate that the new age became fully articulate in song a year or two prior to the war. The genuine poets of high rank and established reputation were obviously little inspired by the war. The Poet-laureate—laureate by native right and general acclaim of the poets, as well as by Royal Letters Patent—wrote few poems under its spell (much to the disgust and fury of that paladin of Archpatriots, Mr. Horatio Bottomley), and evidently even fewer still which Mr. Bottomley studied or understood. Mr. Kipling, like Dr. Bridges, wrote one thin book, *The Years Between*, which, for the most part, in spite of sacred circumstances and one or two memorable verses, suggested only that the quasi-official tribal bard " had kindly obliged as usual." Sir Henry Newbolt's *St. George's Day* was even slighter, though of charming quality in its minor manner. Mr. Binyon (aided by Sir Edward Elgar) moved us once or twice. Mr. Masefield wrote only one poem of the war, and that was no war-poem : like Thomas Hardy's noble words at this time, and the whimsical sentiment of Barrie's plays of the war, and Robert Bridges' anthology, *The Spirit of Man*, it would find more favour with pacifists than with the chauvinists. The same may be said of A. E.'s poems, and Mr. Yeats's references were of the slightest and not at all direct or popular. Even Mr. A. E. Housman has long kept silence and hardly broke it now. What is of even greater significance is the fact that the new men, the Georgians themselves, were not largely war-created artists, nor—if we consider how closely the campaigns touched them personally—was the effect of the war upon their work momentous. Rupert Brooke's sonnets—about which Charles Sorley expressed so acute a suspicion —suffer as art just in so far as they do ring of the war-cry. Their exultancy is more fundamental, and must have found outlet in any event. Charles Sorley himself—a hero of twenty years—is revealed by his *Letters* as a soldier of that rare spiritual honesty (hardly found among his elders or out of a very little circle in the army and one or two per cent. of the conscientious objectors) which could feel and say astonishing things about the war and the virtue it was supposed to engender or evoke ; and the war was an extraneous incident to a soul and mind and heart like his, however vitally and refreshingly he was fascinated by its aspects of chivalry, venture and *contemptum diaboli*. He hated fools, as he said. Mr. Sassoon may cast a doubt upon our generalisation, but Mr. Squire's collected *Poems : First Series* confesses that the years " 1914 and 1915 contributed nothing "—and although we shall probably number among our immortal verses his *To a Bull-dog* and Maurice Baring's *In Memoriam A. H.* (*Lord Lucas*), a line or two of Neil Munro's Hebridean laments, and a score or more of other war-poems, there is no case for the contention that the war affected very much one way or another the steady current and kind of our poetry, or that it begat or nourished the Georgian renascence.

But now that renascence is in full chorus, a glorious burden graced by every conceivable variety of descant ; and nothing so thoroughly indicates the greatness latent in it as the fact that while at least a dozen of the new poets would have loomed almost gigantic in the Edwardian days when we pinned our hopes on Stephen Phillips and Mr. Alfred Noyes, we feel to-day that most of them are still experimenting, practising for their great flight. Some may hesitate to endorse this *obiter dictum* as applied to so perfect an artist as Mr. Walter de la Mare already is ; may question, on the other hand, whether Mr. Sassoon can sustain the glow that his righteous indignation and disdain has so finely

kindled in his war-poems; may forlornly shake the
head over the prospect of Mr. Masefield yet setting
his great genius quite free of the temptations that
beset it; may sadly brood on Wilfred Owen, J. E.
Flecker, T. M. Kettle, Edward Thomas, and all
the others of the lost legion—yet there is ground
for confidence that, magnificent as much of the
work already done undoubtedly is, the living poets
named, and Mr. Blunden, Mr. Shanks, Mr. Freeman,
Mr. Drinkwater, Mr. Wilfred Gibson, Mr. Wade-
Gery, Mr. Thomas Moult, and a score besides, will
without exception make great progress yet.

One of them, by the amount of substantial work
he has published and his slight pre-eminence in
age and reputation, has now reached a point at
which some examination of his contribution to
letters less casual than that of a magazine article
is fitting and called for. It is very sure that the
first book devoted to a critical view of the writings
of John Masefield will not be the last; for these
writings are calculated to interest—and, in various
measures and fashions, to disturb—lovers of English
poetry and the critics and controversialists (to say
nothing of the commentators) for many a day. At
the very least, all such discussion is useful in that
it never fails to attract some (were it but a few)
more to the perusal of what may well prove to be a
source of delight and spiritual profit to them, which
else they might not have reached or thought to assay.

In his cynical reminiscences *Set Down in Malice*
(1918)—a volume of unexpected dullness and somewhat disagreeable in its personalities—Mr. Gerald
Cumberland has referred to Mr. Masefield:

John Masefield has an invincible picturesqueness—a
picturesqueness that stamps him at once as different from

his fellows. He is tall, straight and blue-eyed, with a complexion as clear as a child's. His eyes are amazingly shy . . . his manner is shy . . . you feel his sensitiveness and you admire the dignity that is at once its outcome and its protection.

There are many legends about Masefield : he is the kind of figure that gives rise to legends ; and as he is studiously reticent . . . some of the most extravagant of these legends have persisted and have, for many people, become true. But the bare facts of his life are interesting enough. As a young man he grew sick of life, the kind of life he was living, and went to sea as a sailor before the mast. He had neither friends nor money. . . . The necessity to earn a living drove him into many adventures, and it is told that for a time he was a pot-boy in a New York drink-den. Here his work must have been utterly distasteful, but the observing eye and the impressionable brain of the poet were at work the whole time, and one can see clearly in some of Masefield's long narrative poems many evidences of those bitter New York days.

Evidently the poet came later to London, settled in Bloomsbury and made friends with **J. M. Synge.** Later still—after six months' work on the staff of the *Manchester Guardian,* where we are told his " reserve was invulnerable," and he declined the intimacy, but gained the respect, of his fellow-workers—he returned to London to tackle literary work more seriously.

Beyond one or two facts of ordinary domestic interest, even *Who's Who* adds nothing to our biographical data concerning Mr. Masefield. But has he not himself in a poem of great beauty— *Biography*—disclaimed all faith in history as it usually is told, protesting that the really great things in one's life come not with observation like the events pounced upon by the chronicler ? To

mark the height achieved, the main result

—which is all that the text-books attempt—is not
to tell the story of any soul ; and for Mr. Masefield,
far more than any event to which a historian would
promptly clap a date are " golden instants and
bright days " when some rich emotion bedewed
and freshened his soul :

> The day on which beneath an arching sail
> I saw the Cordilleras and gave hail

or

> The night alone near water when I heard
> All the sea's spirit spoken by a bird

—and the gifts of life that made him what he is :

> The gift of country life, near hills and woods
> Where happy waters sing in solitudes ;
> The gift of being near ships, of seeing each day
> A city of ships with great ships under weigh ;
> The great street paved with water, filled with shipping
> And all the world's flags flying and seagulls dipping.
>
> Yet when I am dust my penman may not know
> Those water-trampling ships which made me glow,
> But think my wonder mad and fail to find
> Their glory, even dimly, from my mind,
> And yet they made me.

And indeed ships and the sea, as well as men and
books and cities, and the wild-rose-lined lanes of
England must have gone largely to the making of
Masefield. With the probable exception of Mr.
Joseph Conrad—that one glorious romantic among
our living novelists—he is the greatest living artist
of the sea ; and the glory of it, with every detail
pondered on and imagined afresh, floods in deluges
of beauty in page after page of novels like *Captain
Margaret, Multitude and Solitude,* and *Lost Endeavour,*
in his early histories of *Sea-Life in Nelson's Time* and

On the Spanish Main, in later works of history like his noble saga of *Gallipoli,* in short poems like *Biography, Ships, The Wanderer, The River,* in some early lyrics and *Salt-Water Ballads,* in his little epic of Philip's Armada, and, above all, in his long narrative poem of *Dauber,* which—whatever be its faults—is filled with the witchery and wonder, the beauty and the sorrow of the sea in all its moods of calm or storm. These reveal his intimacy with the sea and with life at sea. To judge by them, this shy, reserved, sad-countenanced poet may very well have toiled before the mast. Not of imagination alone could a *Dauber* be wrought. Its energy and aching activity, its vivid speed, give eloquent telling of years under the discipline of hardship at sea. Only, if we so argue, we may very well indeed add to the poet's biography the support that *The Everlasting Mercy* gives to the rumour of his experiences in the New York saloon ; and certainly none but a strong athlete and runner could have written or conceived Saul Kane's tremendous sprint with the whole town after him in that same remarkable poem. Again, the volume on *Shakespeare* suggests minute intimacy with the technique of the stage ; and the author of *Reynard the Fox* must surely know at first hand pretty well all that there is to be known about fox-hunting, while his breathless *Right Royal* might as well convince us that steeplechasing has been his pastime from boyhood. This much may be said— he is the poet of real life in its sturdiest, most English, energy ; he writes about real things, strenuous things—always strenuously, and as a rule with healthy realism—and since the days of Chaucer's *Prologue* nothing in English has so captured the very breath of the open field and the open sea as some of his loving, minute descriptions of them both. Nor has any since Chaucer sketched with such lightning artistry English types and English character. Even William Morris, with all his consummate gift of decoration, comes far behind Masefield in Chaucer-discipleship so far as this open-air atmosphere is concerned and in portraiture. Cowper and Goldsmith, who lacked his gift of narrative in verse, had as much of these as he.

But this is to begin at the wrong end of the story. These long narrative poems are thus far undoubtedly Mr. Masefield's strongest claim to fame and regard—but he wrote other verse, not without grace, before he turned to them; and at intervals since—in his deeply reflective *Lollingdon Downs* sonnets, for instance—he has worked in an entirely different verse medium with no little effect. Not only so—he has been more than a poet. A novelist, a playwright, a journalist, a historian, a lecturer, an orator, an editor, a critic—he has been each in turn; and nothing that he has touched—however indubitable his failure in it—has been left without power or quite without grace.

II

EARLY VERSE AND PROSE

THE motive prompting this book is, quite frankly,
a desire to justify the delight obviously brought to
a host of readers by Mr. Masefield's work, and to
introduce his writings to some who do not know
them as a whole; and because of this, quotation
and mere commentary will have a place in it, and
its argument and style will be simple throughout.
But it has a critical purpose none the less. ˙ Justice
never can be done to artistic work by unquestioning
admiration and praise. The more it charms us and
the more its first apprehension pleasantly moves
us, the more keenly should we turn to scrutinise,
to question. If the glory of the first meeting be
just and due, it will be heightened and intensified
by this austerity. True, nothing can well be sweeter
to taste or savour than the bewildering, uncritical
rapture of our first looking into Keats, Tennyson,
The Earthly Paradise, Bridges' *Shorter Poems*, *A
Shropshire Lad*, *The Wind Among the Reeds*—to
name but a few of our youthful intoxications—
and to dwell in the new light with which that rapture
clothes the very landscape and bathes the nascent
imagination. It is a right good thing for a while
to surrender to it wholly; but only for a while.
The purer the ore, the less it need fear to be tested
for alloy; and it is well that our idolatry should

be purged of all that is tawdry, febrile, conventional
or sentimental, that faults in the object of our
delight should be ruthlessly seen and, if possible,
separated from it that it may shine undimmed by
these. For they cannot hope always to deceive or
enchant, and the more unreasoningly they are overlooked the sterner—and perhaps more unreasoning
—will the reaction of revolt be. Witness the altogether undiscriminating aversion to-day from the
Tennyson whose good and bad alike was once lauded
out of measure. So clear-eyed and strong-headed a
youthful critic as the late Charles Sorley [1] passed
quickly from his first idolatry of Mr. Masefield's
every comma. Some of us take longer because we
think less, but the process is invariable and sure ;
and even if it be not completed by any one of us,
others—fresher, younger and more iconoclastic than
we—will but the more unsparingly begin criticising
where we leave off, till the work is at last ruthlessly
done and the way cleared for an estimate of what
alone is precious. But that last recovery is a hard
passage—too hard, very often, even for very worthy
work to achieve. Hence the peril of overpraise and
uncritical connivance at the flaws in the new-created
art which we adore.

Because of this, our very pleasure in Mr. Masefield's
poetry has a right to demand of us that we examine
its quality, appraise the workmanship critically,
review current estimates of the writer's achievement
and seek to reveal what in his art is essential and
abiding and significant.

Without more ado, we may turn to the little bundle
of Mr. Masefield's earliest books in verse and prose

[1] *The Letters of Charles Sorley* (Cambridge University Press, 1919).

—the experiments of his boyhood and youth, in which we see him really merely sharpening his tools, breaking out in would-be original anarchies which, after all, are but imitations and conventional, albeit full of promise. *Salt-Water Ballads* appeared in 1902. No doubt it dazzled its young writer by its daring, its realism, its originality. But it is the purest Kipling, slightly exaggerated and embroidered with quaintnesses borrowed from elsewhere. He devises to do for the lowly human ruffians of the ocean-tramp service what Kipling has done for the slightly more straitly disciplined lower ranks of the British armies in his wonderful ranting song-books, and sets himself the conscious aim of becoming the laureate, the mouth-piece, the champion, the propitiation for the bottom dog of sea life. He states it in the opening poem, called *A Consecration*:

Not of the princes and prelates with periwigged charioteers
Riding triumphantly laurelled to lap the fat of the years,—
Rather the scorned—the rejected—the men hemmed in with
    the spears : . . .

Not the ruler for me, but the ranker, the tramp of the road,
The slave with the sack on his shoulders pricked on with
    the goad,
The man with too weighty a burden, too weary a load . . .

Theirs be the music, the colour, the glory, the gold ;
Mine be a handful of ashes, a mouthful of mould.
Of the maimed, of the halt and the blind in the rain and
    the cold—

Of these shall my songs be fashioned, my tales be told.
                                                    AMEN.

And when he sets to work he fairly out-Kiplings Kipling. The intended realism—though it is really

highly conventional underneath, in spite of itself—
is laid on thick to shock the prim and prudish
and proper : as in *Cape Horn Gospel II* :

Jake was a dirty Dago lad, an' he gave the skipper chin,
An' the skipper up an' took him a crack with an iron
    belaying pin
Which stiffened him out a rusty corp, as pretty as you could
    wish
An' then we shovelled him up in a sack an' dumped him
    to the fish.
    That was jest arter we'd got sail on her

Josey slipped from the tops'l-yard an' bust his bloody back
(Which comes from playing the giddy goat an' leavin' go
    the jack) ;
We lashed his chips in clouts of sail an' ballasted him with
    stones,
" The Lord hath taken away," we says, an' we give him
    to Davy Jones.
    An' that was afore we were up with the Line.

Joe were chippin' a rusty plate a-squattin' upon the deck,
An' all the watch he had the sun a singein' him on the neck,
An' forrard he falls at last, he does, an' he lets his mallet go,
Dead as a nail with a calenture, an' that was the end of Joe.
    An' that was just afore we made the Plate.

All o' the rest were sailor-men, an' it come to rain an'
    squall,
An' then it was halliards, sheets, an' tacks " clue up, an'
    let go all."
We snugged her down an' hove her to, an' the old contrairy
    cuss
Started a plate, an' settled an' sank, an' that was the end
    of us.

We slopped around on coops an' planks in the cold an' in
    the dark,
An' Bill were drowned, an' Tom were ate by a swine of a
    cruel shark,

An' a mail-boat reskied Harry an' I (which comed of pious prayers),
Which brings me here a-kickin' my heels in the port of Buenos Ayres.

I'm bound for home in the *Oronook*, in a suit of looted duds,
A D.B.S. a-earnin' a stake by helpin' peelin' spuds,
An' if ever I fetch to Prince's Stage an' sets my feet ashore,
You bet your hide that there I stay, an' follers the sea no more.

Indirectly it may slightly fulfil the vow of the *Consecration* quoted. But there is room for doubt whether compassion dominates the singer so much as the thought that here is a right good swinging metre, a fine subject for setting in startling musical words and a bluff breezy bad-old-or-young-man-of-the-sea-ishness : a matter of art and æsthetic far more than of social morals or human emotion. And in the same spirit, it is relished by readers— and hugely relished. It is the facile rime of one who as yet knows nothing of the elemental spirit and the tragedy that are found in *Dauber*. It is almost a light-hearted jest, a comic chanty of the sort that sailors are supposed to have sung in olden days— but intended, perhaps, for something deeper than that.

But it is not all such artificial overreaching at grim horror and tragedy. There are lots of tender things like this too in the book—musical in its still artificial pensivity :

THE WEST WIND.

It's a warm wind, the west wind, full of birds' cries ;
I never hear the west wind but tears are in my eyes.
For it comes from the west lands, the old brown hills,
And April's in the west wind, and daffodils.

It's a fine land, the west land, for hearts as tired as mine,
Apple orchards blossom there, and the air's like wine.
There is cool green grass there, where men may lie at rest,
And the thrushes are in song there, fluting from the nest.

" Will ye not come home, brother ? ye have been long away,
It's April, and blossom time, and white is the may ;
And bright is the sun, brother, and warm is the rain,—
Will ye not come home, brother, home to us again ?

" The young corn is green, brother, where the rabbits run,
It's blue sky, and white clouds, and warm rain and sun.
It's song to a man's soul, brother, fire to a man's brain,
To hear the wild bees and see the merry spring again.

" Larks are singing in the west, brother, above the green
        wheat,
So will ye not come home, brother, and rest your tired feet ?
I've a balm for bruised hearts, brother, sleep for aching eyes,"
Says the warm wind, the west wind, full of birds' cries.

It's the white road westwards is the road I must tread
To the green grass, the cool grass, and rest for heart and head,
To the violets and the warm hearts and the thrushes' song,
In the fine land, the west land, the land where I belong.

Perhaps it all has the thin flippant fragrancy of
forgotten favourites of ballroom music and melody
—the waltzes of twenty-five years ago. ` If so, a
word from *Multitude and Solitude* may be apposite :
" Let no one despise dance music. It is the music
which breaks the heart. It is full of lights and scents,
the laughter of pretty women and youth's triumph.
To the man or woman who has failed in life the
sound of such music is bitter. It is youth reproaching
age. It indicates the anti-climax." But there is
more in the flavour of this song and the many like
it—the colour of country gardens full of old-fashioned
hardy perennial flowers in glory of colour and opu-

lence of bloom, the clean fragrance of rosemary
and lavender and leaves laid up among old cuttings
of them, a wistful tuneful melancholy, a gracious
old-world affectation.

When we turn to the second little verse-book,
Ballads and Songs, this wistful tunefulness and the
same careful carelessness of rhythm prevail.   In
both his arts—prose and verse—the artist has now
fallen under the spell of a much more delicate genius
than Kipling's.   It is Yeats, Yeats, Yeats everywhere and all the time, or nearly ; the magic singer
—who alas ! has sung so little since those days—
of the Celtic Twilight, of Kathleen ni Houlihan,
the mystic Ireland of his dreams, the Secret Rose
of Beauty.   We are reminded of the Irish master's
music on every page, even though, as Dixon Scott
put it, the younger bard goes out on clandestine
raids in all quarters and gathers a little hoard of
trinkets, coins, doubloons, and gems to reset cunningly
and fascinatingly in his own verse. He may not
know it—but it is still all precious imitation.   One
feels that if Aedh had never sung of the Rose in
His Heart in *The Wind Among the Reeds*, we should
not be greeted by a bonny opening verse like this :

Would I could win some quiet and rest, and a little ease,
In the cool grey hush of the dusk, in the dim green place of
    the trees,
Where the birds are singing, singing, singing, crying aloud
The song of the red, red rose that blossoms beyond the seas.

And when

> The bells they chime and jangle
> From dawn to afternoon

our thoughts go back to Shropshire and the Bredon
Hill of Mr. Housman.   But indeed there is a quaint

distillation of all the Pre-Raphaelite fragrancies
through many a verse as

> They rhyme and chime and mingle,
> They pulse and boom and beat,
> And the laughing bells are gentle
> And the mournful bells are sweet

And this effect is increased by the Pre-Raphaelite
mannerism of introducing a quaint old vernacular
word out of a ballad :

> Oh, who are the men that ring them,
> The bells of San Marie,
> Oh, who but sonsie seamen
> Come in from over sea.

Back to Yeats and the curlew calling in *The Sorrow
of Mydath* :

> Weary the cry of the wind is, weary the sea,
> Weary the heart and the mind and the body of me,
> Would I were out of it, done with it, would I could be
> A white gull crying along the desolate sands.

At all events it is a very fair imitation of the more
obvious charm of the Yeatsian verse. It is little
more than an echo of that, and when the next verse
begins

> Outcast, derelict soul in a body accurst,

we feel that this is arrant rhetoric, ludicrously
if unconsciously insincere, a second-rate lover-in-
Maud parody of emotions the writer has never felt
nor deeply imagined. But even in the gentle plain-
tiveness of the less forced lines the poet is not so
appreciative of the stern intellectual strength, the

sensitive economy of words, the severe restraint that go to the making of Mr. Yeats's delicate pieces of beauty. Deliberate reverie and striving after atmosphere are by no means enough.

Indeed, it has to be confessed that the best things in the book—the nearest to perfect—are the merest trifles; the pretty jingles of rime and curiosities of design like the well-known *Cargoes,* which cannot boast one finite verb.

> Quinquereme of Nineveh from distant Ophir
> Rowing home to haven in sunny Palestine,
>   With a cargo of ivory,
>   And apes and peacocks
> Sandalwood, cedarwood and sweet white wine.
>
> Stately Spanish galleon coming from the isthmus,
> Dipping through the Tropics by the palm-green shores,
>   With a cargo of diamonds,
>   Emeralds, amethysts,
> Topazes, and cinnamon, and gold moidores.
>
> Dirty British coaster with a salt-caked smoke stack
> Butting through the Channel in the mad March days,
>   With a cargo of Tyne coal,
>   Road-rails, pig-lead,
> Firewood, iron-ware and cheap tin trays.

Such verses, were they never so perfect, must of need be minor—mere exercises in word-colouring. There is a loftier ring in *Fragments,* and a sterner control of language for all the Kiplingese:

> Troy Town is covered up with weeds
> The rabbits and the pismires brood
> On broken gold, and shards, and beads
> Where Priam's ancient palace stood. . .

Once there were merry days in Troy,
  Her chimneys smoked with cooking meals,
The passing chariots did annoy
  The sunning housewives at their wheels

And many a lovely Trojan maid
  Set Trojan lads to lovely things ;
The game of life was nobly played,
  They played the game like Queens and Kings.

So that when Troy had greatly passed
  In one red roaring fiery coal,
The courts the Grecians overcast
  Became a city in the soul.

And later in the same song what a gallant lilt is
heard as he sings of ancient mythical cities and their
glory, and of how

Men in desert places, men
  Abandoned, broken, sick with fears,
Rose singing, swung their swords agen,
  And laughed and died among the spears

Sea Fever, too, is a genuine lyric ; Mr. Masefield is
always at his best on the sea : and in *C. L. M.* the
touching, manly-boyish verses on a mother's grave,
with which he poignantly supported the agitation
for women's franchise, appear some of the essentials
of great and sincere poetry, moral and tragic
attributes, seldom found in these early books.

The poems quoted and referred to show verse
more restrained in one way than that of *Salt-Water
Ballads*, more highly decorative in another, less
callow, more serious and reflective, more concerned
with the beauty of Love than with the grimness
and stark horrors of Death ; but still, at best, only
a very skilful discipleship of other older cunning

artists. There is a good deal of rum-tiddle-tum—
"rhythmically circling in a little silver setting of
sound." The singer has nothing of his own to say
yet, and no style of his own. He is simply making
pretty things—and he could hardly do better, it
may be, if only he avoid vanity over such conceits
as he may produce—gems though they be. Little
room enow for vanity! Had this been all his gift,
one can almost hear the high Georgian disdain of a
decade and a half later summing up all that he has
as yet achieved. "A pseudo-Celt run to seed"
does it say? "He had, no doubt, a measure of
skill, an ear, some feeling, an eye—but where is
the brain, the nerve, the breath of the Immortal,
in it all? Let him rest in peace. Oblivion come
gently on him, but come it must."

One must add more rigorously, however, that
really even this earlier Masefield can be very irritating
in his imitativeness. Some of us without his genius
came no less under the spell of Mr. Yeats in our
boyhood's effusions and remember the bristling
wrath that all unexpected confronted us when we
showed them to his admirers. We can well understand their indignation over us when nowadays we
find ourselves tingling with anger as we read—or
try to read—some of this abler youth's deliciously
clever imitations : especially in prose which posi-
tively reeks of *The Secret Rose* drenched in some
alien perfume. The very strangeness and sweetness
of Yeats's qualities render him the more impossible
as a model. A young writer should dare to be
himself from the very beginning, and never imi-
tate the masters he admires. It is the only way
to honourable achievement. Certainly the great
apostles of beauty must influence him, to the core

of his soul; but it is no noble form of adoration to
copy their gestures. What we love most in them
we love least to see repeated by others. Indeed, we
cannot tolerate such pious mimicry. It nauseates
and enrages us, puts our literary backs up with a
more-than-feline distaste. Parody is a delightful,
if a "not wholly admirable," art: unconscious
parody is very apt to be mere miry sentimentalism;
and Mr. Masefield's two early books of prose, *A
Mainsail Haul* (1905) and *A Tarpaulin Muster*
(1907), so minutely fashioned with exquisite preciosity, are full of dandified use of turns of speech
such as those with which Yeats and Synge had caught
and charmed the ear of the age. One would write
with reverence of even the schoolboy exercises of
the poet who was to write *Dauber*, but when we
find a sketch beginning thus—

"The seals is pretty when they do be playing," said the
old woman. "Ah, I seen them frisking their tails till you'd
think it was rocks with the seas beating on them, the time
the storm's on"—

we do feel naturally something of the exasperation
which assails one when a mannikin of some eight
years talks wise, using—as if they were his own—
words he has heard grown-ups say. Who is this,
we demand (insolent though we be!), who struts at
the Cross of Kiltartan, or somersaults it on the
Aran Islands? Placing ourselves on a high pedestal
as critics, we call it precocious and quite too pettily
self-conscious to be allowed in Art.

And here again—although it is so fairly, so cunningly, so meticulously fashioned; so entrancingly,
if only we had not read *Rosa Alchemica*—this typical
passage from *The Yarn of Lanky Job* is the undiluted

3

early Yeatsian affectation mimicked to the letter. The spiritual, as well as the literary idiom, is appropriated—as far as that can be. Lanky Job, we learn, was a lazy Bristol sailor, notorious for his sleepiness throughout the seven seas.

One day he was lolling on a bollard on the quay at Bristol as fast asleep as man could wish. He had fallen asleep in the forenoon, but when he woke the sun was setting, and right in front of him, moored to the quay, was the most marvellous ship that ever went through water. She was bluff-bowed and squat, with a great castle in her bows and five poops, no less, one above the other at her starn. And outside her bulwarks there were painted screens, all scarlet and blue and green, with ships painted on them, and burning birds and ladies in cloth of gold. And then above them were rows of hammocks covered with a white piece of linen. And every little poop had a rail. And her buckets were green, and in every bucket there were roses growing. And the masts were of ebony with mast-rings of silver. And her decks were all done in parquet-work in green and white woods, and the man who did the caulking had caulked the deck-seams with red tar, for he was a master of his trade. And the cabins was all glorious to behold with carving, and sweet to smell, like oranges. And right astern she carried a great gold lantern with a big blue banner underneath it, and an ivory staff to the whole, all carved by a Chinaman.

The later volume, *A Tarpaulin Muster*, is worse instead of better. It is spoiled by too much writing about writing—an infallible symptom of artistic and intellectual poverty or impoverishment, as Mr. George Moore says of *The Secret Rose* itself. We see it in the opening story, *Edward Herries*, as the hero tinkers at his sonnet; or as thus, upon his lady's portrait

" I have lived in moonlight," he thought. " My world has been white like moonlight and pure like moonlight.

Now over the valley comes the sun, golden like corn, bounteous as July. Now, my beloved, my beauty, my share of God upon earth, your knight goes out into the sun."

We also hear of one windy March day " when the beauty of the wild weather seemed to have passed into her blood," and about " the sword of her beauty hacking the brambles from his soul."

> " I am fallen among the brambles," he sighed.
> " I am blackened and ashamed."

His " mind burned with the memory of her beauty."

Some memories always appear (another sketch tells us) " significant like certain dreams " and likewise " as direct revelations of something too great for human comprehension." " The rhythm of rowing, like all rhythm, such as dancing or poetry, or music, had taken me beyond myself " ; and so, of course,

> We were eternal things, rowing slowly through space, upon some unfathomable errand, such as the Sphinx might send to some occult power, guarded by winged bulls in old Chaldea.

For of a truth " within the ivory gate, and well without it, one is safe ; but perhaps one must not peep through the opening when it hangs for a little while ajar," and beyond a doubt " I should have liked to have seen those stately pale women, in their black robes, with the scarlet roses in their hair, swaying slowly. . . ." And " all the others repented with the fervour of primitive people " " where immortal things still trouble the peace of mortals."

And on, on, on it goes. One wants to shout

" Hurrah, Yeats ! Yeats again " after a while, as
one watches for this new sort of cliché. It becomes
intolerable, nearly intolerable—although if we had
not read *The Celtic Twilight, The Secret Rose,* and
Ideas of Good and Evil we might have enjoyed this
novel exotic perfumery and cadence, and, even in
the act of condemning it, we acknowledge that it
is the fact that fifteen years ago we did it ourselves,
as much indeed but never as well, that has made
us thus ribald about it. *O Pulchritudo . . . sero
te amavi!* Of course, everyone who writes—or hopes
to—has to learn in some such way. All young
poets—or very nearly all—do it, age after age.
Tennyson, Swinburne, Mr. Yeats, and now Mr.
Masefield himself, and Mr. de la Mare, have had their
slavish bondsmen and idolators. But of how few
men of letters can it be said that their very experiments, their juvenilities, their imitative stages,
retain for later days the interest and even the
tarnished beauty that these boyish tricks of Masefield's still have for us ?   After all, even of
Shakespeare and his Sonnets, one of our sanest
judges has written :

> The theme at first seems artificial and no doubt it was ;
> the wise artist chooses an artificial theme when he is too young
> to get one from his own experience, for he knows that he
> must learn his art before he can use his experience of life
> in it. Besides, the young artist delights in his art for its
> own sake ; it is still a pleasant game to him, and he is content
> that others should make the rules of it. Thus the young
> Shakespeare was glad to write like the other poets of the
> time . . .[1]

Yet as surely as increasing age there comes to the
artist a time when that game is up, when he sees

[1] A. Clutton-Brock, *Essays on Books* (1920).

that he has only been trifling artificially with other men's music, and producing what in his vexation he may call "mere pretty-prettiness."

It is always with a sharp pang that one recognises this—and ninety-nine per cent. of us, who once saw ourselves in fancy crowned with the laureate's bays (or scorning them!) never lift our head or our voice again—more wisely than cravenly, it may be. We are ashamed and mortified. We may surrender our allegiance to Literature, and seek other ploys for life. At all events, and at all costs, we have to chuck all this mouthing of insincere imitation, this spurious mintage of loveliness. Of course, what we really need—whether we are to be poets, or something else—is some form of impassioned and painful experience, some real unfeigned suffering, mental or spiritual probably, that will shake and batter us into stark honesty and sincerity of style sure enough and fast enough ; an experience that will make us shrink from all expression until the Holy Spirit itself—whatever be Its name—takes us up and forces us to utter what is now in us, cleanses our lips with a fiery stone from off the altar and opens our closed mouth to make confession meet and to sing because we must. It might be called the religious crisis of life—using "religious" in the widest sense.

There is spiritual agony and exaltation in that experience. It is not to be sought ; it cannot be simulated long without detection, though—most unhappily—such insincerity is sometimes attempted, and poetic pretenders, self-doomed to perdition in fame, capacity and soul, are never few. There can be no art without sincerity, and a great ultimate inner constraint upon the Spirit of Man.

And the transition is surely painful. Not all at once does the poet leap to his artistic power, the caterpillar to the butterfly. Minerva may spring full-armed from the brain of Jove—but the born poet must also be made. Like the ship in Kipling's tale, he has to " find himself " and cease to be a conglomeration of separate pieces and compartments. He must suffer.

III

THE NOVELS

THIS book is avowedly unbiographical. *Causeurs*
have remarked upon Mr. Masefield's reticence. The
story of his life is no concern of ours, or of the world's,
as yet. If more than that were wanting, we have
his own wise theory of life in *Biography* to dissuade
us from any endeavour to trace its details, even
from a hope to illuminate his poems by these. On
the other hand, it is neither intrusively impertinent
nor otherwise illegitimate to deduce in general the
presence of struggle and passion in the poet's life
from his poems and other works. Imaginative
agonies, at all events, must have been his who wrote
The Street of To-day, *The Everlasting Mercy*, and
Dauber.

Many of the hinted adventures by land and sea
which the maturer works are held to suggest must
have taken place in the years between the making
of these fastidious-seeming but really all too facile
early pieces of bric-à-brac, those mosaics of quaint
and pretty things, and the inspiration of *The Everlasting Mercy* with which he startled the whole
world suddenly in 1911. He had been studying the
life of men with grave, sad eye in many a strange
and humble corner—life outwardly disreputable
enough very often, but never meaningless.

In the interval he had not been idle as a man of

letters; and in the novels and plays that fill those
years we can see him groping after a new medium,
a new expression—experimenting as wonderfully as
ever, making a powerful impression by all his work,
and yet somehow never reaching success in it, and
showing traces of bitterness (though not the deeper
embitterment) because of failure, failure to find
the message and the meaning of this cruelly blotted
and cruelly chequered mortal life and the world
of men and women.

In the disgust and nausea of discovering that one
is not yet authentic poet, most writers abandon
verse for prose; and so did Masefield—although I
suspect that much of his *Lollingdon Downs* sonnets
and his *Philip the King* volume may have been
meditated and made about this time; for they do
not always conceal traces of the old Yeatsian
influence.

He took to writing novels; and although, in reply
to a question not long since, he told me that he
"could not remember in what order they appeared,
but it does not matter much since they are all
(I hope) forgotten by now," I hold them a far from
uninteresting or unimportant series.

"Here's a fellow!" we said, when we read his first
attempts at fiction proper as distinguished from the
earlier lyrical prose—for they were full of thought
and conscious artistry of a quite new kind, a stern
philosophy of life, a gospel of endurance, a facing
of facts known and facts unknown. There was a
panting eagerness in his prose style too—a real
discovery in technique.

And yet, looking back, we see that he was
struggling with something he could not master.
He had invented a truly magnificent "verbal

machine that applied all his energies creatively,
stamping a pattern on knowledge, giving a design
to reality, minting memories into talismans that
gave new heart and courage to other men and
other writers "—and yet none of them is an unquali-
fied success : far from it. And, sad to say, just
because they are such honest aims at something
far above commercial fiction, their comparative
failure is intensified, and I suppose they perhaps do
not attract their readers so much as the cheap,
vivid trash of the average pot-boiler would.

Nevertheless, *Captain Margaret* (1908) is magnificent, superb, with some pages of radiant beauty.
It is a story of action, and not altogether unworthy
to be thought of along with *Treasure Island, Taken
from the Enemy,* or *Fort Amity.* Charles Margaret,
a gallant English gentleman and poet, owner of the
sloop *Broken Heart*—so named from his disappointment in love—has decided upon an adventure of
trading and colonising on the Spanish main along
with his friend Ned Perrin and his captain—an old
buccaneer named Cammock. As luck will have it,
however, Olivia, his lost love, and Tom Stukeley,
her coarse and criminal husband (a man " wanted "
for debt, forgery, and darker deeds), are in Salcombe,
the port from which he is to sail ; and in spite of
all protest, nothing will serve Margaret but that
he should pay his farewell respects to the lady.
He does so and sets sail. Stukeley, however, being
in a very tight corner, devises, on hearing from his
wife of Margaret's plans, to row out to the vessel
and so to escape. Olivia—very much in love with
her husband's quality of certainty, though he has
already tired of her and her refinement—is beguiled
by his cock-and-bull story of his desire " to help

the Indians " against their Spanish oppressors,
and together with a boat's crew they board the
Broken Heart, pursued by shot and king's officers.
The firing upon Olivia so stirs Margaret that he
braves the law, receives and defends the fugitives,
and escapes with them. Olivia, who is rather stupid
—one must own—is deceived by the chivalry of
Captain Margaret and allowed to believe in the
blackguard who has won her; even the firing is
explained away; but Stukeley's swinish insolence
aboard ship becomes wellnigh intolerable. He
saves his skin by pleading falsely that Olivia is
enceinte. At Jamestown, it is only by the connivance
of the Governor, a friend of Captain Margaret's,
that the company escape arrest and a swift journey
to the gallows in England; after securing, however,
the best of the season's tobacco crop. Stukeley,
unfaithful to his wife, and a breeder of mutiny aboard
ship, ultimately betrays the whole expedition in a
mission to Tolu, himself escapes, joins the Spaniards,
marries a Spanish wife, and dies of plague on the
very morning of a quixotic attempt by Margaret
to secure his rescue for Olivia's sake. The awful
scenes of the sack of Tolu, which Margaret is unable
to prevent his allies from carrying out, and the
counter-attack by the Spaniards, in which he almost
perishes, and the desertion of his crew, shatter for
ever the idealist's dreams of a virgin city dedicated
to his lost lady. Her eyes, meanwhile, have been
opened to all—to Stukeley's beastliness and to
Margaret's nobility—and her assurance to the latter
that his city is builded in her heart leaves us at
the end of the book with the conviction that they
will marry and make life a fairer thing even yet
in Old England.

It is, as has been said, a story of action ; and
in dealing with action, vigour, enterprise, the writer
does magnificently. The fighting is splendid, the
very sickness of fighting is noble. The browbeating
by Stukeley, the toleration of Stukeley, and the
putting of Stukeley in his place in due course has
a fine thrill and dignity of telling. The sea scenes
—the breaking of Mr. Iles, or the chaffering at
Jamestown, for example—and many of the descriptions of ports and rivers and islands, are excellent.
But the story teller cannot manage his characters.
He is not so prone as Gissing to explain parentheti-
cally what the characters themselves and their actions
should reveal—but he is not quite free from this
flaw. A much more serious lack is the power to
create the illusion of vitality in his persons. For
nine of the twelve chapters Olivia is indeed a very
dull doll and quite incredibly stupid, and all the
reveries about Beauty, the lapses into sheer vague
twilight Celticism—the old spurious aping of Yeats's
more obvious mannerism—do not evoke the slightest
conviction that she is more. It is only after her
disillusion that she becomes at all a noble creation.
One cannot help feeling that only by exaggerating
the childishness and silliness of the heroine could
the hero, for all his delicate dignity and courtly
grace, be made a tragic figure ; and that, for this
same necessary end, even Stukeley is made a human
beast of iniquity quite beyond all reason or credi-
bility. Nothing vile is forgotten—as some details
had better have been—to paint his rottenness.
But for his physique, he might even suggest Huish
in *The Ebb-tide*. But the feeling will not away that
he has been specially manufactured, that the screw
is ever and anon being given another turn to keep

up the horror and disgust, that it is all a contrivance,
an invention, a device, a trick—not the truth of
life, or anything like it. Besides this, whenever Mr.
Masefield turns from actions to philosophy the same
mooning sentimentalism is apt to creep confusingly
over all and the people think and say some grotesquely
inane things. All power disappears in colourless
lifeless reverie. It is invariably thus when the
Celtic twilight is borrowed, or when moralisings
upon the ubiquitous and very indefinite Beauty
occur.

A beautiful thing is a vigorous form of life and all forms
of life have parasites. The parasites don't attach themselves to the things you speak of because the things are
beautiful. . . . I think that all these things are images in
an intellect. By brooding on them, one passes into that
intellect.

Or this, of Olivia :

All sweet and lovely and gracious things had wrought
her ; but they had not fitted her for this. Something was
wrong with the justice of the world ; for surely such as she
should have been spared. She was not for the world ; not
at least for the world of men. She was the idea of woman ;
she should have been spared the lot of women.

Or again, the preciosity of this nullifies its worth
for a tale of the kind :

But he had loved her, he had seen her, he had been
filled with her beauty as a cup with wine. He would carry
her memory into the waste places of the world. Perhaps
in the new Athens, over yonder, among the magnolia bloom
and the smell of logwood blossom, he would make her memory
immortal in some poem, some tragedy, something to be
chanted by many voices, amid the burning of precious gums
and the hush of the theatre.

There are some epithets that catch the sense vividly
—a " hawky pounce," for instance. And epigrams
of worth are to be found—

He was a cad, born a gentleman.

St. George became John Bull directly he had killed the
dragon.

—even if sometimes fine moralisings are somewhat
" dragged in."

Sometimes I feel that if a man thinks with sufficient
strength, he really makes a sort of intellectual guard about
himself. I mean, as faith saved the men in the furnace.

The songs were all vile. They were the product of dirty
drinking-bars, and dirty young men. Youth sometimes
affects such songs, and such haunts, from that greed for
life which is youth's great charm and peril. That men of
mature experience should sing them, enjoying them, after
tasting of life's bounty, was hateful, and also pitiful, as
though a dog should eat a child.

The bitterness so pervasive of *The Street of To-day*
only occasionally and faintly tinges these moralisings,
however.

There are minor traces of carelessness, no doubt.
The time of the action is plain enough for all needs ;
but it is slightly bewildering to read of old women
" who remembered King James " and later on to
find a King James very much to the fore. And it
is a pity that loose punctuation should be suffered,
with this result upon a compliment to the heroine :

" My God, though, Edward, do think what she is, think
of her life. Think what. To have her husband driven in
a cart and hanged." " Yes. But it's surely a worse tragedy
for him not to be hanged, and to go on living with her."

It is all the more astounding when we remember
that the same speakers are enthusiastically addicted
to the reading of Campion and Donne amid all their
harassing troubles. It is idle and ungracious to
pick holes like these in this book. It is full of faults,
no doubt. It is immature. Its style is garish
enough at times for all its strength. Its positive
weaknesses are sufficient to debar it from ranking
with romances that it naturally enough recalls to
us. Yet for the sake of certain pages one would
desire not to forget *Captain Margaret*, nor to let it
be forgotten.

Even less, perhaps, would one part with *Multitude
and Solitude*, which followed it in 1909. There are
great thrills in it—among others, one of the most
terrible tropical storms in literature—and, if you like,
it is a novel about twentieth-century science : far
enough away, surely, from the sentimentalities and
voluptuous affectations that Masefield was unfit, too
unsophisticated, to steer amidst. The hero is Roger
Naldrett, a writer of drama. Because of its sincere
and advanced attitude to morals, the play on which
he has spent his genius is hissed off the stage. The
scene recalls the *Playboy of the Western World's*
reception. Seeking a steadying power in the clear
mind of his Irish lady-love, he crosses to her home
only to learn that she has been drowned in a Channel
disaster. The mental upheaval induced and fur-
thered by these two overwhelming blows comes to
equilibrium in a scientific expedition to Central
Africa with a friend who is making a study of sleeping-
sickness. The expedition meets with calamity. All
its members fall victims—but by a lucky guess or
chance (which suggests the weak side of Masefield's
plots) Naldrett discovers an anti-toxin and saves his

friend's life in the article of death, his own also
and the others; and returns home restored in soul.

It is a good story—quite well written—with some
magnificent chapters and noble social indignations.
It has no love interest—at least, the beloved is dead
—and this may remove it from the ordinary classifica-
tion. Perhaps it is easier to manage a story without
female characters, and in this one there is no
harassing preoccupation with sex (mental as well
as physical) such as makes *The Street of To-day*
so torturing a study and which one feels to be as
yet quite beyond the power of the author of *Captain
Margaret* to contemplate with adequate appreciation.
On the whole, *Multitude and Solitude* is the most
perfect of Mr. Masefield's novels. *Captain Margaret*,
for all its gallantry and beauties, is boyish, crude;
The Street of To-day over-intense and over-elaborate.
This is juster and better. But even so, one feels
that here Masefield is somehow not working in his
proper medium. He is trying to do another work
than his own; one in which he is an outsider. So
long as he is dealing with facts, narrative—fighting,
scenery—he is splendid. But philosophy, theory,
sociology? No; these are not for him, though his
conclusion that " science is not a substitute for
religion, but religion of a very deep and austere
kind " is arresting enough.

The same verdict must be given—albeit reluctantly
—about *The Street of To-day* (1911), although there
are great things on almost every page. Several of
the persons of its predecessor meet us again in it.
It is the story of a wooing and an unsuccessful
marriage, a rather tragic journey to the House of
To-morrow by way of the mistakes made and dis-
covered in the Street of To-day. It is almost entirely

devoid of action—conversation, very brilliant and
often irrelevant conversation, is the chief means of
unfolding plot and characters—and as Masefield's
charm is greatest among life's bustle and intenser
activities, the result is just what might be expected.
The book is stodgy and heavy. It is not dramatic.
But it has qualities that no other book of its author's
has. It breathes the very air of modern move-
ments. It tackles sex-psychology and the mental
make-up of the three chief characters—Lionel
Heseltine, Rhoda, and Mary Drummond—with
desperate and profound earnestness and with much
philosophic, if not artistic, success. It is one of the
most literal studies of journalistic life ever written.
But in every respect it *is* " a study." It is a picture
of London, studied and seen as a gigantic social
misery, a cancer, a great incurable disease that has
got ahead of all surgery with its crowds of folk
themselves for germs. But Masefield is not at home
in it. It must have been agony to conceive and
write such a book. To read it is hardly less. The
seer cannot pierce the veil of filth and misery to
the reality, the beauty, the soul, which he believes
to exist behind it ; and these things so revolt him
—especially in his study of the somehow incompatible
temperaments of Lionel and Rhoda, their spiritual
sex-antagonism—that he plunges again into vague
utterance and the course of the book is not clear
and the work as a whole lacks fascination, although
it has so many ideas, so many sayings, so many
pages nobler by far than the best of the fiction of
the market-place at its best can give us. Mr. Arnold
Bennett complains that he found it difficult to read,
and it certainly lacks the last touch of mastery. It
is alert, intelligent, earnest, sincere, generous, careful

—but it is also, for one thing, needlessly long and spun out. One is tempted to " skip " incessantly. It is clogged by excellent brilliant irrelevant small-talk and miscellaneous information. It is like the expanded contents of a notebook in which the author had noted down materials of all kinds for future plays and poems, and in it lie some tales of pity quite fit to be rendered up in verse to rival *The Widow in the Bye Street*, such as the story of John Dent in chapter x.—a chapter written in the minute, placid vein that Miss Una Silberrad, in her Quaker stories among others, can manage (or once could) so very much better than anyone else. Mr. Masefield, however, is apt to become tautologous and maundering in this vein with his " valerian and rhubarb tart " touches and quasi-lyrical style. Preachy passages again are lugged in. Careless touches—like " ophthalmic eyes " and " a life like she had led of old "—are discoverable : and even a poet in the making, it seems, is capable of this :

She had known that he cared for her, for her intimate essential self, the little inside soul that made the jelly of her eyes alive.

On the other hand, there are epigrams innumerable, and all very pointed and clever :

One-eyed men think that all the two-eyed see double.

Success is the brand on the brow for aiming low.

There'll be a view at the top. That's what you always get for dilating the heart—a complete sense of the beauty you've abandoned.

Prison kills the fineness in a man so that the weakness in him may rot.

4

The Normans among us have never quite mixed with the Saxons. They have only learned to build worse.

Perhaps a man who saw Shakespeare went to America.

There are many ways of changing the world, and they all seem so innocent till it's too late to stop them.

Christ comes as Anti-Christ, always.

There's only one way of getting a reform—by making the alternative dangerous.

But the artist's taste is grievously lacking at times, or a humourless loathing has made him reckless. The hero in the very second chapter tells a lady, " It makes your hat like a great big flower : I should think people want to pick you." And why must the author tell us quite seriously that " In the bathroom Lionel felt inclined to strip and bathe " ? or that " a hair-brush had been left for him. He saw that it was a woman's brush, ' Thoughtful of them,' he thought, wondering, an instant later, if the thoughtfulness had been implanted in them by brothers or lovers. He would not use the brush. He would as soon have used another person's tooth-brush. He preened with a pocket-comb. At lunch he held forth on the beauty of Feasts of Purification " ? Or can a new-made bridegroom really be imagined talking thus to his bride ?—

" Rhoda, you're wondering what men are like. They're very like women. Only they pass their lives in a playing field, while you pass yours in a boudoir looking on. You mustn't be afraid of me. You're just as big a mystery to me, as I am to you. And I'm just as much afraid of you, as you are of me. . . . We have to teach each other," *et cetera, ad nauseam.*

"Will you come with me, Rhoda?" He was drawing her out of the quarry into a glowing world. She nodded, swallowing.

(O swallow, swallow!) It recalls *The Yellow Claw*, by Sax Rohmer!

Finally, when Rhoda almost immediately and somewhat inexplicably (so far as we are shown) reacts violently against everything in matrimony —she is a superficial, hypochondriac, malignant little creature; made in that mould, as usual, to heighten the dignity and manlike perplexity of the very callow and impossible hero—she does so in passages that read like a parody of Masefield by the inveterate Mr. J. C. Squire. Here is one:

All through her illness he had been under the microscope of a narrow nature. He did not love her as she wanted to be loved. How could she love him? Little deadnesses in him, little failures in responsion and understanding, grew intense now. They hurt. They swelled the distaste to an antipathy. She had loved that thing. Now she saw him. That thing had held her in his arms, kissing her, here, in this very house. He was her husband, with rights over her. Once, as she lay on that sofa, he had bent down and kissed her throat. The memory of that kiss forced her to another seat. How could she wipe away from her all the stains of those memories? They made her feel unclean. All the room was foul with memories of him. The memory that he had sat there was like his presence there. Feeling contaminated, she drew up a creepy-stool. "Dora doesn't understand," she thought bitterly. "She thinks it's only my illness. It's a revolt of me."

And there are dozens more like it. The novel is contemporary with the more hysterical phase of the feminist agitation just prior to the war with Germany, after which the services of Britain's women were rewarded (too late!) with the franchise, and

under the mental strain it becomes as extravagant
and hysterical and obsessed as many of the most
sensitive souls—both women and men—were apt to
do at that time. There was no calm and no peace
in England then, and tendencies to cynicism and to
fanaticism opposed each other with cruel extremity
and grew by opposition. It is more than reflected
in this novel with its fierce humourless earnestness,
its acute anti-war emotion, its endless verbiage,
its unpleasant gloom, and its forced loathing and
its bitter accuracy in description of domestic circumstances of strain which must, one fancies, occur in
almost all homes sometimes and cause disaster
unless the gifts of humour and a gentle tongue are
possessed—as they happily are as a rule among
ordinary people. But the people here are not
ordinary—they are unreal, unnatural, fabricated.
Wit in abundance is theirs, but only in Mary Drummond—and rarely in her—is there a gleam of humour.
It is clear that the writer's mind is growing bitter,
unsympathetic. All, perhaps, because of too near
a view. The perspective of life is distorted. He
cannot see humanity quite clearly enough to portray
it and interpret it in this form. He may see torments
plainly as Dostoevsky; unlike Dostoevsky, he cannot see beyond them. His own soul is growing
and passing through a painful stage of growth—
not inaptly paralleled by Lionel's struggle to establish
his newspapers and sociological aims, or by the
rather needless but terribly real trials and vagaries
of the Heseltines in their efforts to achieve harmonious
justice in their home-life. He too suffers from the
prevalent disabling lack of humour—the very names
he gives people and papers suggest it; the *Back-
wash, Snip-Snap,* Sir Pica Galley—and it may be

that it is that lack that accounts for his final failure
as novelist, even as it leads to disruption in the
Heseltine establishment, to brutal spite on Rhoda's
part, and wellnigh to suicide on Lionel's. Such in
very truth may be the artist's transition from imitator
to creator, from artificer to artist, from sentimentalist
to seer ; the battle of an artistic soul to find itself,
to develop and mature its creative power if it have
any, suffering all the wounds of the soul and barely
escaping some of its potent poisons. The mind is
not yet ripe, and the process of its evolution is
accompanied by agony of soul. It is not surprising
that there is much confusion and fumbling in this
novel written out of so perturbed and rended a
bosom. It is a book so patient and minute and
faithful in its desperately serious study that it was
bound to hold something of great truth and value.
One could wish it a wide circulation among young
newly-weds—preferably those with the saving sense
of humour—who happen to be unaware that marriage
is a vocation and an education with some passages
hard to construe. Perhaps it might increase—or,
in some cases, even create—the desirable sense of
humour : for at times it is indeed a little ridiculous.
The same faults mar it as literature almost inevitably.
The writer is working in a foreign element. But
there is much that is delightful in it, and the poet's
quality peeps out at times in radiant beauty. As
in the closing words :

Life is a wild flame. It flickers, the wind blows it, the
tides drown it. Perfect life, or that which we on earth call
God, is no thunderous thing, clothed in the lightning, but
something lovely and unshaken in the mind, in the minds
about us, that burns like a star for us to march by, through
all the night of the soul.

Landscape, too, is beginning to bring the mind to its true gifts, even though the metaphysics and technique of landscape never leave us free to enjoy the writer's art.

We ought to live in places where the will to live clothes itself in lovely shapes. The good spirits haunt those places, the gentle souls. A place expresses the quality of the spirits which seek life there. Sensitiveness to that quality makes landscape art endurable. Men must not ask of a landscape artist the number of the trees nor the pattern of his colours. They must ask him where to raise the altar to the genius loci.

Wherever love, or hate, or joy has been, the spirit of the earth is coloured. We walk in a subtle air which takes colour from our intensity. Those who follow in our paths sense suddenly the rosiness or blackness of the places where we have felt. Our lives are creating spirits which will haunt the ways we have trodden.

Nothing in this kind is too high to hope for from a writer capable of elegiac beauty like this:

They stared together at the view. They saw it as the rooks saw it, from the heights, with nothing above them but clouds bowling on the blue. Bowling aloft there, so near, so very near, they were strangely like the bows of ships. Ships making a bubble, nosing deep into it, white to the rail. The softness of the white was another tenderness to the minds of the watchers. And beyond that softness was the blue, infinitely bright and gentle, an intense, glad flame of blue. The wind made a noise in the grove. The trees bowed a little, giving to the blast, with a shivering of touching branches. The branches were not in leaf. There was a dustiness of buds upon them. They were at that moment when the beauty of the branch against the sky has that other beauty of the beginning leaf upon it. Far down below in the valley, England was at peace. The fields were like the lands in a map. Smoke marked the villages. A spire stood out. Drowcester Cathedral tower glowed out white like a lighthouse. Cows in a meadow called. Their moving was like the ploughed field speaking. The air was an intoxication with the laughter of blackbirds. Up there on the hill, the sense of possession filled the heart. The landscape was a heritage displayed. One owns only what the imagination grasps. Here for a moment the imagination glowed with the visions of immense possession. And with this came an exultation of being thrust far up, by the power of the earth, into the cup of the sky, into a life new and strange, fiery, and of a new glory.

But one can't permit too much of this in a narrative, and it would take more of this charm of landscape than can be permitted to save a book in which the hero has taken twenty pages of the twelfth chapter to say " Rhoda, darling ! "

The author might have gone on and written more and better novels, as critics—Mr. Arnold Bennett among them—expected. But he wrote no more : for his other stories—*Martin Hyde the Duke's Messenger*, *Lost Endeavour*, and *Jim Davis*—are mere tales of adventure for boys. *Lost Endeavour*— the best known of them by reason of its publication in Nelson's cheap series—beginning breezily enough, wanders away into romantic lands and simply loses itself there until the author grows tired of it and claps on a conclusion " just anyhow." It was probably written for the most part long before it was published, and, if it be not impeaching Mr. Masefield's artistic integrity, one may express the suspicion that it obtained resurrection only because the author's new fame made publishers not only willing but eager to publish anything he had to give them. It is just an exercise in writing—with some extraordinary blunders of construction in it (for example, a footnote occurs in what is given for a *spoken* narrative—part ii. chapter xv.) ; with much of the old persistent mimicry of Yeats's *Secret Rose* mannerism :

> I could not help feeling that she had been delicate and beautiful with the high, austere, wise beauty of those who pass their time meditating upon spiritual matters, etc., etc.

Yet with much waste of beauty in it too, for all that.

IV

THE CRITIC AND THE HISTORIAN

BUT all this time Mr. Masefield had been experimenting in other fields than fiction. He wrote plays also. And if critical insight is of any worth to a playwright, we might have expected him to succeed in dramatic creation—for his little book on *Shakespeare* in the "Home University Library" is a unique primer and a masterpiece of its kind. Nothing fresher has even been written of the plays, although the compass of the little essays is necessarily narrow.

It is a digression to turn aside at this stage to Mr. Masefield as critic ; but some brief notice must be given of his work in this art, and of his early essays in another realm also.

For our note on his criticism we shall confine ourselves to his book on *Shakespeare*. He has been generous with "introductions" to the works of other writers (if that is a virtue), and his prefatory essays—e.g. to the *Chronicles of the Pilgrim Fathers* in "Everyman's Library"—are worthy writings. He wrote a personal recollection of Synge and a centenary essay on Ruskin. He has also contributed countless fugitive pieces of criticism to newspapers and reviews, but his laconic reply to an inquiry concerning them was, " Blessed be he who spares those stones." The little volume on *Shakespeare*, however, better than any other, gives ample taste of his quality; and the first feature that impresses one is its freshness. A generation ago, university professors of English literature complained with justice that ninety-nine per cent. of their students in essays and examination-papers on Shakespeare simply borrowed or paraphrased Dowden; in our own day, Dowden had been superseded by Professor A. C. Bradley, and to some extent by Sir Walter Raleigh; and the dramatic critics, on the whole, were little better than the undergraduates in this regard. That Ruskin in *Sesame and Lilies* had praised Shakespeare's heroines and (with faint praise) King Henry V and Valentine—was assumed, as a rule, to be enough. Mr. Masefield, however, is true to himself and snaps his fingers at Ruskin so far as that goes (although he has written finely of Ruskin the Prophet too, in the volume of Centenary studies edited by Mr. J. H. Whitehouse):

Shakespeare seldom allows a woman a great, tragical scene. Cleopatra is the only Shakespearian woman who dies heroically upon the stage. Henry V is the one commonplace man in the eight (historical) plays. He alone enjoys success and worldly happiness . . . wooes his bride like a butcher, and jokes among his men like a groom . . . accuses Scroop of cruelty and ingratitude and forgets those friends whom his own cruelty has betrayed to death and dishonour. He has a liking for knocks. Courage tempered by stupidity (as in Fluellen, etc.) is what he loves in a man. He, himself, has plenty of his favourite quality . . . a common man whose incapacity for feeling enables him to change his habits whenever interest bids him.

Slight as the essays are, they are compact of thoughtfulness and imaginative reading. They differ from

most academic studies of Shakespeare in their keen
eye for stage-technique and suggest that the critic
has a first-hand knowledge of this.

He is no foolish idolator, as some are. He sees
Juliet become "a deceitful, scheming ' liar,' less
frantic, but not less devoted than her lover," and
on *Titus Andronicus* he grimly writes : " There can
be no doubt that Shakespeare wrote a little of this
tragedy ; it is not known when ; nor why. Poets
do not sin against their art unless they are in desperate
want. Shakespeare certainly never touched this
job for love."

In nothing, however, does the poet's insight declare
itself so powerfully as in the justice it metes to those
favourites of Shakespeare's deep heart commonly
designed by our commonplace thought as his " vil-
lains." That Shylock is the man of brain, battling
to uphold intellect in a boorish world that cannot
be generous to intellect in any age, is no new judgment—however little known by the casual reader or
spectator ; but there is something bigger, something
fundamental, in Masefield's insistence upon another
than the easy popular verdict on the unsuccessful
in general :

In the historical plays, Shakespeare's mind broods on the
idea that our tragical kings failed because they did not conform to a type lower than themselves. Henry V conforms
to type. He has the qualities that impress the bourgeoisie.
He is a success. Henry VI does not conform to type. He
has the qualities of the Christian mystic. He is stabbed in
the Tower. Edward IV conforms to type. He has the
qualities that impress the rabble. He is a success. Richard II
does not conform to type. He is a man of ideas. He is
done to death at Pomfret. King John does not conform to
type. His intellect is bigger than his capacity for affairs.
He is poisoned by a monk at Swinstead. Richard II fails

because, like other rare things, he is not common. The world cares little for the rare and the interesting . . . The soul that suffers more than other souls is little regarded here.

The charm of the book is its quiet pointing out of unsuspected and overlooked beauties in the great dramatist's work, beauties seen by the critic's own mental eye, and not obvious to the many ; like the scenes in the last acts of *Richard II* which reveal the mind of the deposed king ; the calling down of the curses in the third scene of *Richard III*—the contrast of which with the theatre's modern scenes makes the critic anxious for the nation's soul ; the tragedy that occurs when a woman like Katherina is born with a manly soul ; the church scene in *Much Ado About Nothing*, the majesty of verse in *Julius Cæsar*, the grandeur of thought in *Troilus and Cressida*, the poignancy of Othello's cry—

It is the very error of the moon, &c.;

the fierce imaginative energy of *King Lear*, and the joy when heart-break is poured at last on the misery of the " excessive terrible soul " of the old king ; the splendour of vision in *Macbeth*, and the " fateful re-echoing" galloping of horse in Act IV, scene i. ; the ring of personal hatred for the " flunkey mind," and of " the servile insolent-mob mind " in *Coriolanus*; the terrible scenes of shame reproving the persistence even now of so ancient a foulness in the fourth act of *Pericles*, and the lovely sea-scenes in the same play.

It is a gratuitous effort to criticise at length the criticisms by a writer in our appraisal of that writer's own creative work. But one other fact must be noted : his elucidation of the reading of life and history given by Shakespeare—that life must not be altered violently, as the tragic flaw in every character tends to alter it. Hamlet, Coriolanus, Othello, all reveal this lesson. " To Nature, progress, though it be infinitesimal, must be a progress of the whole mass, not a sudden darting out of one quality or one member "—so that the pioneer, the idealist, must suffer and become a centre of tragedy, and there's an end on't, no matter how noble the obsession. Life seeks to preserve a balance and all obsessions, by upsetting the balance, betray life to evil. At the best it is the Cross of humanity, the price of progress and disciples ; often alas ! the price of failure to progress, or to inspire discipleship. " Tragedy," he sums up, in comment upon *Lear*, " is a looking at fate for a lesson in deportment on life's scaffold. If we find the lesson painful, how shall we face the event ? "

About Mr. Masefield's earlier essays in history little need be said here. His researches in the lore of buccaneering must have been prodigious, as the sketches of pirate captains in *A Mainsail Haul* and that rare book *On the Spanish Main* make manifest ; and they are graphically displayed. John Ward, John Jennings, John Coxon, and Robert Knox (from whom Defoe got many ideas for *Robinson Crusoe*) " are straight our friends " ; men who have faced big issues of life and death for months together, and are wise with a rough and noble wisdom ; though occasionally some of them " have their riches in the sinks and cellars of Fame's temple." We have already seen some of the breed in *Captain Margaret*, and although the sketches are worked up into a thoroughly artistic literary form, they are, on the whole, the stuff of literature rather than literature's self.

Little more can be said of *Sea-Life in Nelson's Time*. It is an admirably careful thesis based on painstaking and extraordinarily minute historical research, and set down by a golden pen ; but it is a work of science rather than of art, although it is full of material for artistic treatment, and no doubt its making was part of the preparation for *Dauber*. It does not belong to the same category as *Gallipoli*, which is a saga no less than a history.

V

THE PLAYS

WE have glanced at Mr. Masefield's critical study of Shakespeare's thought and drama, and now must turn to his own plays, especially those written during the period of transition already defined. Although it is always a serious error to read autobiography into an author's dramatis personæ, except in the sense in which all work is autobiography, one can deduce quite plainly from *Multitude and Solitude* that Mr. Masefield had at this period immortal longings after the craft of a playwright also. The reviews of Naldrett's unlucky play in chapter iii. show that he appreciated that side of the game and was more conscious than usual of its wry humour. The talk of Heseltine and Naldrett in chapter vii. is also illuminative of his ideas and ideals :

" Yes. I'd give the world to be able to write. To write poetry. Or I'd like to be able to write a play. You see, what I believe is that this generation is full of all sorts of energy which ought not to be applied to dying things. I would like to write a poem on the right application of energy. That is the important thing nowadays. The English have lots of energy, and so much of it is wasted. . . . Don't you find writing awfully interesting ? "

" I find it makes the world more interesting. Writing lets one into life. But when I meet a man like yourself I realize that it isn't a perfect life for a man. It isn't active enough. . . ."

And again :

" I want to be quite sure of certain elements in myself,
before I settle down to a literary life. Nowadays a man
writes because he has read, or because he is idle, or greedy,
or vicious, or vain, for a dozen different reasons ; but very
seldom because his whole life has been turned inward by
the discipline of action, thought, or suffering. I am not
sure of myself. Jacob Boehme was right. We are watery
people. Without action we are stagnant. If you sit down
to write, day after day, for months on end, you can feel
the scum growing on your mind. . . . I sometimes feel that
all the thoroughly good artists, like Dürer, Shakespeare,
Michael Angelo, Dante, all of them, sit in judgment on the
lesser artists when they die. I think they forgive bad art,
because they know how jolly difficult art of any kind is.
I don't believe that art was ever easy to anybody, except
perhaps to women, whose whole lives are art. But they
would never forgive faults of character or of life. They
would exact a high strain of conduct, mercilessly. Good
God, Heseltine, it seems to me terrible that a man should
be permitted to write a play before he has risked his life
for another, or for the State."

It is not necessary for our present purpose to
examine all the plays minutely ; and what little we
have to say about those more recently published
may as well be said first.

Good Friday (1916) is a little morality in rimed
verse on the Passion-day of Jesus. It begins with
a calm austerity of style which is properly impressive,
but it is almost completely spoiled by the intrusion
of a symbolic madman with his song of pennies—
rather a weak reminiscence, I have sometimes
thought, of the Fool in Yeats's beautiful *Hour-
Glass*. It is marred, too, by a few of those
slovenly touches which occur occasionally in Mr.
Masefield's work.

PILATE. Tell Caius Severus that I want him.
[*Exit* SERVANT.
So. [*To* CHIEF CITIZEN.]
What I have written, I have written. Go.
[*Exit* CHIEF CITIZEN. PILATE *watches him.*

It recalls some of Stephen Phillips' cruder lines:
as these slightly savour of his better :

> a cry, no spoken word
> But crying, and a horror, and a sense
> Of one poor man's naked intelligence
> Pitted against the world and being crushed.

The darkness reddening to a glare as Pilate enters
is another of the stagey touches dear to Phillips.
The ballad-songs introduced are woefully out of
harmony with the spirit of the play, and the events
passing. Indeed the dragging in of songs couched
in utterly inappropriate phrases must be looked on
as a recurring Masefieldism in the plays ; notably
here and in *Pompey the Great*. But the account of
the Crucifixion recited to Pilate by Longinus is
moving and awful by its very simplicity, and—
considering that it is written in riming verse—must
be accounted specially wonderful.

> The two thieves jeered at him. Then it grew dark,
> Till the noon sun was dwindled to a spark,
> And one by one the mocking mouths fell still.
> We were alone on the accursed hill
> And we were still, not even the dice clicked,
> Only the heavy blood-gouts dropped and ticked
> On to the stone ; the hill is all bald stone.
> And now and then the hangers gave a groan.
> Up in the dark, three shapes with arms outspread.
> The blood-drops spat to show how slow they bled.
> They rose up black against the ghastly sky.
> God, lord, it is a slow way to make die

5

A man, a strong man, who can beget men.
Then there would come another groan, and then
One of those thieves (tough cameleers those two)
Would curse the teacher from lips bitten through,
And the other bid him let the teacher be.
I have stood much, but this thing daunted me :
The dark, the livid light, and long, long groans
One on another, coming from their bones.
And it got darker and a glare began
Like the sky burning up above the man—
The hangman's squad stood easy on their spears
And the air moaned, and women were in tears,
While still between his groans the robber cursed
The sky was grim : it seemed about to burst.
Hours had passed : they seemed like awful days.

In general the description is dignified and fine, and the supreme day is helpfully visualised. On the other hand there is no striking revelation or interpretation of Pilate where several are possible to any thoughtful student. The madman, like the old grandfather in *Nan*, becomes a nuisance. He is in no wise akin in fantasy to Feste or the Fool in *Lear*, or even to Teigue in Mr. Yeats's perfect morality play.

The Sweeps of Ninety-Eight, a little rebel comedy written in 1905, and *The Locked Chest*, written in 1906, were published in 1916. They call for no special comment. The latter play has a spice of tragedy in it ; the earlier is a rollicking comedy composed—it is best to believe—around conventional ay-figures. Both are pleasant enough, but insignificant : mere trifles, curtain-raisers.

The Faithful (1915) is a very different matter. It is a Japanese tragedy of three Acts, written in the mixed manner. It has beautiful directness and a

lofty spirit of heroism. It slips into Elizabethan
mannerisms at times, and shows the influence of
Hamlet and of Webster's plays. It has the breadth,
the ennobling atmosphere and dignity of these
spacious dramas. Nowhere, certainly, does Mr.
Masefield show more happily his sympathy with all
spiritual triumphs, however tragically attended, than
in this play. Asano, a Japanese nobleman who is
being insidiously robbed of his ancestral lands by
Kira, an upstart, is deluded by the latter (who has
to instruct him in Court ritual) into the unpardonable
breach of etiquette of striking him in presence of
an Imperial envoy, and suffers death. The play
tells finely how Kurano, his counsellor, and his
peasants vow to avenge him ; how, after a year of
suffering and moving self-sacrifice, they keep their
vow, requiring Kira to kill himself, and despatching
him when he shirks the issue ; and how at the
command of the royal herald they cheerfully—even
exultantly—kill themselves.

It is a tale of most moving loyalty, and the ring
of joy in the closing scene " belongs to an order of
tragedy of which the West knows nothing." We
have nothing to compare it with ; but in spite of
every reason to expect otherwise, it is dramatic
through and through, and on the stage would probably be more successful than any other play of
Masefield's, even the melodramatic *Tragedy of Nan.*
The severe and beautiful language—utterly delivered
from sentimentality—would be powerful indeed if
spoken by beautiful voices, and the play fulfils the
requirements of tragedy in a degree impossible to
Nan and unachieved by *Pompey.* It is astonishing
that it has had relatively little attention bestowed
on it. Of course, its manner *is* mixed—the cold

Japanese convention does not easily blend with
the full-blooded Elizabethan traits and such episodes
as Kurano's simulated madness in Act II. The
death of Asano in the end of the first Act with a
lyric of strange delicacy on his lips removes him
from the hero's *rôle*, which really pertains to his
tribe, but apart from the conflict of dramatic systems
the play is wellnigh flawless. It is so utterly unlike
anything else that Mr. Masefield has done that one
wonders what unique and never-to-be-repeated dream
gave it him, and how he remembered it so clearly
on waking as to write it down so well. Here, for
once, the lyrics are organic to the play, except the
Elizabethan " Wine is a strong drink, Beauty is a
stronger," and the speech throughout is in keeping
with the serenity of ritual pervading the action.
It throbs with unpretended passion and with pathos
all the keener for its lofty restraint. It brims with
heroism. Kurano's pledge recalls the appeal of
Garibaldi to young Italy, without any sense of
parody or weakness :

> KURANO. Let me trap no one. There will be no feasting
> in this fellowship, only a wandering in the cold, perhaps
> for months, and death at the end, according to this
> decree. Understand solemnly that the man who puts
> hand on mine marks himself for death.
> VOICES. We will come, lord Kurano.
> VOICES. We know what the end will be.

The heroic thrill streams through the simple words
again and again, perfect in power and effect. " My
lad, we are not like other people, who can enjoy
themselves. We were born knights, with duties."
" Evil is very strong, but men that will give their
lives are stronger." " We will go into the wilderness

with what we believe "; and the poignancy of the lyrics is not felt the less because of the exaltations of self-abandonment and the adoring loyalty pervading the whole.

Death took away my friend; and I have prayed for years,
But Death has paid no heed. Death does not yield to tears.

> Once very long ago
> When there was still the sun,
> Before these times, before
> The light was darkened,
> One whom we used to know
> Made life most noble; one
> Who would have changed the world
> Had people hearkened.
>
> It was a dream. Perhaps
> Time drugs the soul with dreams
> To all but blind desire
> For high attempt;
> Then the intense string snaps;
> The project seems
> A hearth without a fire,
> A madness dreamt.

Of all his many books so beautifully inscribed "To My Wife" none is so perfect, so unstained, so prideworthy, as this priceless piece of beauty. None of the poems is at once so delicate and so strong. Nothing in his writing, save some passages in *Gallipoli*, can equal it for verve and wonder. It is not characteristic. It stands apart from all the rest. What *The Hour-Glass* is to Mr. Yeats's works, perhaps *The Faithful* is to Mr. Masefield's.

After these digressions we must resume our study of the transition period between the poet's two

poetic phases, which was interrupted at the close
of Chapter III, and examine the two more famous
plays—*Pompey the Great* and *The Tragedy of Nan*
—written and published in the years of the novels.

As drama, *Pompey*—published in 1910, but written
before *Nan*—must be called a failure. It is a mere
succession of telling incidents, a kind of selected
historical chronicle, event leading to event without
resistance or irony. It is fine pageantry, but there is
no tension of interest aroused. The play is simply
a psychological analysis of Pompey's mind—the
mind, rather, of Pompey as conceived by Masefield.
The mighty Roman is figured as a heroic all-but-
pacifist of ancient days trying to avert civil war:
an estimate which, I fear, history does not bear out.
One seems to remember some neatly effectuate
massacres associated with this peaceable Pompey.
But, of course, Mr. Masefield is not to be held respon-
sible for Roman history. Unfortunately, however,
his hero is self-spoiled by priggishness, vacillation,
irresoluteness, reverie, incompetence, by unctuousness
and a high-falutin morality which is not true for
him, and only offends the more because it *is* true
in a deeper sense.

The play has a fine dramatic opening. A myste-
rious voice is heard beyond a balcony of Pompey's
house, warning his servants. "Stamp your foot,
Pompey! Aha! Ha! Pompey!" it cries, echoing
the Consul's boast that if he but stamped his
foot Italy would be filled with soldiers rallying
to his standard. He will need them now—Cæsar
is marching on Rome—and where are they? Then
Masefield misses his great chance—the splendid
clash of temperaments in the opposition of Cæsar
and Pompey, militarist and idealist. But no:

Cæsar never appears. Pompey is not allowed to struggle with him. As in the novels, action, action always, is Masefield's safeguard, philosophy and introspection his peril as an artist. But instead of a struggle with Cæsar, it is Pompey struggling with himself we see—and the result is not drama, although the play is full of tender moments and deeply felt writing. As usual, there is the extraordinary disfiguring carelessness of vulgar and coarse speech mixed up with heroic and singularly lovely lines. The chorus at the end is grotesque, ruinous. And " It's been so nice seeing you " is diction hardly in keeping with a Roman tragedy.

The Tragedy of Nan (1909) is quite another kind of play. It has been staged and has had long successful runs at all the Repertory theatres in the English-speaking world. It is—superficially, at all events—most moving, most powerful emotionally. I have several times seen it played in a great commercial city, and large audiences—including many dozens of stolid prosaic business men in no wise to weeping given—were reduced, yes completely reduced, to tears : whether this be to the praise of the play or contrariwise. On the stage, it impressed me as being nearly as poignant and noble as Thomas Hardy's *Tess of the D'Urbervilles,* and although one recovers from so extravagant a judgment and better detects the poverties of the play on reading it, it is still acutely troubling to the emotional susceptibilities, and it certainly stirs one to anger against cruelty and to deep pity, as tragedy should.

Nan Hardwick is an orphan, a charity girl, whose father has been hanged for sheep-stealing. She is taken in at the house of her Uncle Pargetter, and

the entire Pargetter family—especially the malignant
aunt and her empty-headed, spiteful daughter Jenny
—make life a positive hell for the poor girl. She
bears it meekly, and her lot is lightened by the
love advances of Dick Gurvil, a neighbouring yokel
of a sensual cast, and to him she plights her troth.
But the she-devil, Mrs. Pargetter, is watching events ;
and, wishing Dick to marry her own Jenny, tells
him that Nan's father was hung, and that his own
father will disinherit him if he marries the child of
such an one, and he will die a starved tramp. She
dangles the prospect of a dowry for Jenny before
him, and all too easily—too rapidly for dramatic
verisimilitude, at all events—secures him. In a
scene of most terrible poignancy, Nan learns the
real character of her lover. When she is waiting
for him to speak to her at that evening's family
social party, to acknowledge her as his bride-to-be,
and to " claim her before them all," as he had said, he
joins the rest in brutal jeering at her. Her passion
and agony is terrible, and is heightened rather than
relieved by the maundering poetical talk and half-
witted sympathy of the dotard old grandfather (of
whom we *do* have rather too much). She is left
alone. But by and by Government officials come
in. It has been found that her father was innocent,
and she is given fifty pounds in compensation. The
miserable Dick turns to her again, but she will have
none of it. It is the like of him, utterly selfish and
sensual, who ruin women—more sensitive, more
susceptible, unsuspecting women. She will save those
women, she says, as she stabs him to the heart ;
and we are left to understand that she has gone out
to drown herself.

Justice cannot be done to this pathetic play by

a mere outlining of the plot. I, for one, have judged it a masterpiece—with limitations, of course—and most critics have agreed : though some have not been above making cruelly faithful perversion of it in clever parody. Charles Sorley, one of the great lost legion of our young poets, declared for a time in enviable boyish enthusiasm that " it is finer than *Œdipus* " ! But the critics are not unanimous, even in the main. One of the ablest and most incorruptible of them, Miss Storm Jameson, is absolutely annihilating in her estimate of it, in the resentment of her strong effort to establish a rule and school of criticism which may regain the theatre for art.[1] It is the dregs of an outworn tradition and convention ; it is false-naturalism, mock-Ibsenism, ugly, vicious, maudlin, commonplace and brutal. The love scene at the opening of the second Act— which I thought, and still think, one of the finest in recent drama (a peer of that in Synge's *Playboy*, also condemned by Miss Jameson)—is disagreeable and degrading. Nan, whom I thought amazingly queenly in her humble suffering patience, occasions resentful disgust by her unrestraint as she talks to her mean and stupid lover, whom she is to stab with a pastry knife, " of blood and hell like a decadent poet of foul things." Her finest words—and less savage critics, like Mr. Shanks, feel there is something in this—are *not* the words of a peasant. For the rest, her talk is unpleasant raving. " An ugly story : two mean and silly women, a foul-mouthed sensual youth, an insensate old man, and a hysterical girl are its characters. The language is either below common decency, or strained out of all semblance to reality. It is not tragedy, because not one of

[1] *Modern Drama in Europe* (Collins, 1920).

its people was worth a moment's thought; it is not art, having neither beauty of form, nor greatness of content. It remains a tale of evil, most evilly told, fairly typical of a belated Naturalism, a thing ' most foul, strange, and unnatural.' "

Well, *there* we have it! And it does shake any confidence in one's own critical faculty, for Miss Jameson's book is a masterly and much-needed thesis, and she can praise generously once in a way, though she is so contemptuous of Masefield and Yeats, and none too kind to Synge. It is pleasant to read her estimate of Barrie's pity and courage. No doubt there is point in some of her shattering criticism of *Nan*. Yet one can't but feel that all this "langwidge" is rather ill-tempered—that this terrific intellectual Nietzschean is surely rather an highbrow, rather a superior person, rather snobbish, too, in her dealing of judgment.

No doubt the characters and the love scene are both rough and primitive, and touched with the fragrance of the soil, but the play does have a rustic tenderness too, something of the purity of passionate truth, and when well acted it commands the sympathies powerfully, and, as I have said, it certainly evokes a passionate indignation against the brutality it depicts. That, I think, does justify it ethically; and artistically too, I believe, for it could not move even that anger—or stir us as it does when Nan finds her coat flung into the hogwash, for example —had not the poet given us some beauty for all these ashes. As for the finer speeches being out of character—with deference to Miss Jameson and to the more merciful critics who utter the same accusation—I must maintain that the charge is preposterous, absurd. The most notable instance is Nan's heart-wrung speech to Dick in Act III, when he is endeavouring to ingratiate himself afresh with her.

> DICK. I was.—O, I can't. To show that I 'ad done with yer. I was angry.
> NAN. Because I didn't tell you of my dad?
> DICK. Yes.
> NAN. There be three times, Dick, when no woman can speak. Beautiful times. When 'er 'ears 'er lover, and when 'er gives 'erself, and when 'er little one is born. You—you'd have been the first to stop me if I'd spoken then.

The scarcely-veiled snobbery that allows no possibility of tragic worth to such as Nan attempts to justify itself by as unreasonably denying her these words. They are " not the words of a peasant girl." Are they not?

" The poor are often very refined," said Perrin, in *Captain Margaret.* " The very poor. Especially in the country."

Does Tess use no such speech? And why should not the lowliest peasant girl, having so recently endured all that Nan has endured, rise to tremulous achings of emotion and passionate beautiful speech in such an hour? It will not do for these pre-eminent critics to condemn her to be vulgar and then blame her for being vulgar. To rob her of her tragic truth and then deny her a place in her own tragedy. As for the inherent probability of the speech : I have repeatedly heard fishermen pray, in little meetings held for open prayer, in language unborrowed and unstereotyped, but worthy of Isaiah, and with passion unfeigned, whom I yet knew to be capable of lewd and lurid oaths upon the harbour-wall, and of very flagrantly dishonest income-tax returns. I heard them very often, and such prayer-eloquence was a frequent exaltation of emotion induced, no doubt, by the peril and the anxious worry attending their calling and by " His wonders in the deep." As for the less delicate speech and poor Nan's " unrestraint "—do critics not have enough humour to remember that they can witness no scene of the kind in actuality, that they become so needlessly bitter about a scene of which no lover or beloved will ever question the fitness and the fairness ? *Nan* may not touch the tops of tragedy ; but it is a slice of life, revealingly interpreted, a brave plea for womankind, even if tinged with the same hysterical pressure as is so doggedly fought in *The Street of To-day*, and the central figure is certainly undeserving of Miss Jameson's implacable rage and strictures.

On the other hand, there is no figure comparable with Nan in *The Campden Wonder*, a little play in three scenes, produced in 1907 and published in the same volume (along with a single-scene sequel, *Mrs. Harrison*), and this gruesome piece helps one to understand Miss Jameson's rigour better, and to concede much to it. It is the ghastly tale of a drunken jealous elder son, John Perry, who, to be avenged on his prosperous and industrious younger brother, Dick, bribed with three hundred pounds the brother's master (Mr. Harrison, another drunkard ready to do anything for drink-money) to keep out of the way for a month or two. Meanwhile he made a false confession to the effect that he and his brother and their foolish old mother had together murdered Harrison, the body being hid by the other two in a place unknown to him. This secures the hanging of all three—John, exulting in an insanity of gratified malice, and Dick, in a frenzy of anguish for his wife and little child, on whom starvation and ignominy will now fall. A highly conventional Parson, a stage figure, is depicted in shameful satire, mouthing insincerities of consolation, and glibly applying most sacred Scripture in a manner hardly decent ; and the execution is carried out with crowds and drums. The Parson is sitting in the lock-up, white and sick, when all is over. Mrs. Harrison, who has believed in Dick and Mrs. Perry all along, bursts in with the news that Harrison has returned home that morning. She is under the impression that the execution is fixed for the morrow, and is overcome—as the Parson is—at the discovery that she is too late. In the sequel, however, the overcoming seems to have led her to an orgy of vulgar abuse towards her unspeakable man, who has connived at the murder, yet only so as to turn again—when the outrageous Parson comes across to get at the truth—and back up his muddled story of his having been kidnapped, sold into slavery and set free again. Harrison goes off to church with Parson to give thanks for his restoration, and while they are gone Mrs. Harrison takes a poison, turns to her Bible, and reading it aloud dies on the stage.

Caricature and bathos abound in the play. The invention of the Parson—if one can call it an invention—seems a thoroughgoing piece of unscrupulous parody : not indeed malicious, but a careless taking over of a stock-figure originally drawn with a touch of malice. In the bad old days there may have been unspiritual ecclesiastics of an incompetent type, and the fact may legitimately inspire the sketch of the Reverend Robert Spalding in *The Private Secretary,* but the irresponsible, serious-seeming lampoons

of Drew in *Nan* and this parson, and the gratuitous
involving in scorn and ridicule of the very tender
words they are made to abuse is, at the most generous
estimate, unworthy of so sensitive a genius as gave
us *The Faithful*, and it is in itself harmful to social
morals, and indirectly poisons the attitude of
thousands of casuals towards an institution whose
help they often require, and whose ethical aims
merit their active support. Not ridicule, nor satire,
but something sterner is the only worthy and effective
weapon for the castigation of the base or inefficient
priest. It would be different if the figures were
actual or photographic, but they are as conventional
as the Pantaloon, and it is time that this convention
of calumny were shattered by minute and careful
truth, be it dark or bright. One writes this here
for the sake of Art, no less than in the interests of
Religion and the Churches. I do not think Mr.
Masefield intended to lend himself to the propagation
of this silly misrepresentation, and the retort of a
lack of humour might fairly be made against me,
had the cheap, unworthy gibe of generations borne
no infectious fruit of falsehood in countless impressionable young minds. Anyhow, I have suggested
a windmill for some dramatist (rather than critic)
Quixote's attentions, and shall eagerly await the
presentation for the first time in drama of a bad
parson—a *real* bounder—embodying some credible
accusation that can be challenged and is worth
challenging, or of a good parson who is not an
absolute mug. The lay-figure of la-di-da curate or
vicar should give place to some serious and sincere
study, based on facts that are general rather than
on caricature of selected cases. Immunity from
criticism, or from the demand of an all-but-super-

human standard, no virile son of the Church or priest of religion would desire or welcome. There is room enough for Art to challenge us who would gladly break a lance *pro Christo et Ecclesia.* Our schism—the anti-Catholic practice and attitude of the Catholic, the fissiparous tendencies of Protestantism ; our failure even to face the real problems raised by international and inter-racial relationships and the fundamentals affected by war ; the cowardly fear or incompetence that holds us from facing our own curriculum with its intellectual, doctrinal, moral, social, political and economic (and even artistic) questions ; our members' frequent profession of a faith whose symbol is that of stark and bloody renunciation, coupled with a practice (more or less unconscious) of virtual Hedonism—these are but a few of the subjects admitted to be meet for God's radiant and redemptive scourge of Art. But let there be no caricature, no sneer, over these heartbreaking flaws. Let them be treated with honesty however trenchant, and anger, if you will, and cast out for the monstrous stalking devils they are. But give credit likewise where it is due, and let the portrayal be no localised, one-sided and unfair display. In the social work of the churches and in the pioneer work of missionaries carrying the best (however imperfect it may seem to the superior people who only criticise) that civilisation knows to lands of terror and hate, will be found a heroism second to none—not even the artist's. And the Auld Alliance of Church and Art is a consummation devoutly to be wished for their mutual improvement and cleansing, and for the restoral of health and honesty, devotion, and the grace of adoration, and freedom and catholicity in both. In *The Campden*

Wonder none of the characters is admirable. The play neither exalts the lowly and meek, nor faithfully depicts the beauty and goodness, nor the cruelty and true coarseness of the poor of any age. It is a parody rather. In some moods it would tease the reader into derisive laughter, although the element intended for comic in it tends rather to bore.

But it is possible to detect a few features that might give it on the stage a slight melodramatic appeal to an audience willing to be content with the drama that thrills but the nerves. (That this book should be dedicated to Mr. Yeats would rather stagger us, were it not that certainly there are some beautiful dialect words and speeches fit for beautiful speaking in *Nan*!) Presumably, the very luridness and extravagance of the malice-drunken John Perry's revenge, and the death-drums, have the morbid fascination of a black flag; and in innocent Dick's anguish for his baby girl's future there is the possibility of a histrionic poignancy like that of Nan, and the fervour of the farewell scene might seem less hysterical in a theatre than it does in the study. But there is no one in this play in whom we can love Humanity—and Tragedy demands that—while (against all comers) we continue to champion Nan Hardwick as one who does make us love humanity more.

Neither in novel, then, nor stage play, has our writer "found himself" altogether : but in these works we can increasingly discern signs of that mental passion, traces of that spiritual experience of which I said in the beginning that it knocks all the nonsense, artifice, make-belief, posing, insincerity out of a man ; derides his imitativeness, and either destroys his hope of notable creative power altogether,. or through pain endues him with a song of his own, all his own, and his alone. Whether you seek it in *Nan*, or in *Multitude and Solitude* and *The Street of To-day*, you find evidence that the dreamy lad who used to make fictitious little mouthfuls of his songs out of vagrant fancies, dainty little conceits and baubles of rime and rhythm, trifles that for all their quaint and cunning workmanship show nothing of the soul but its growing pains and its green-sickness (and not much of the former), and the sham pathos of languid dreamy youth, has been stripped of that ; has been forced to see life at first hand in its *true* pathos, its strong and frequent horror, its cruel doubt and real tears, and—through these or not at all—to cut out the path on which he may come again himself, and bring others, to life's joy, delight and truth. It is not ours to discover and trace the secret paths of any soul in the awe and bitter agony of the new birth, of self-discovery and life-discovery ; but we are aware here of an utter revolution, a chaos revolving by and by to a new self-possession and mastery. And now the day is coming when the poet who is poet indeed, not by choice alone, but by fiery calling, is to burst forth with a new song in his mouth.

The new Masefield was a startling apparition in very deed !

VI

THE EVERLASTING MERCY

I SHALL never forget that torrid day in 1911 when I languidly picked up a blue-covered copy of *The English Review* in a smoke-room, sank with it into a basket-chair, lit my pipe, leisurely opened the magazine and got one of the shocks and surprises of my life. It is told of an apocryphal horse-racing parson that, when a dexterous wag had erased the word "tree" and inserted in its stead "horse" in next Sabbath's Psalm in the Church Bible, the sportsman in due course read aloud, "I saw the wicked flourishing like a green bay——" He stared incredulous with bulging eyes. "I saw the wicked," he began again, "I saw the wicked flourishing like a green bay—why, confound it all, it IS 'horse'!" Even so the vocabulary of *The Everlasting Mercy* made *lots* of people sit up, rub purblind eyes. The "room was sudden with horror." At first we gasped "Oh!" What blasphemy! What indecency! Phew! Then, dazed and unbelieving, one read the long poem again—and again—and again. We remembered the violent remark of a character in *Multitude and Solitude* : "The Celt's love of the beautiful is all bunkum." We felt that here was a break away from the weak imitation of Yeats and the Celtic Twilight. It began to dawn on us, though we still had our doubts, and though the poem was

full of glaring obvious flaws, that here was one more
of the world's great sudden original poems and one
of the greatest religious poems ever born. And not
religious only—but a wild defiantly Christian slap
in the face to all sham paganism and all sham
religion, something exceeding the righteousness of
the scribes and Pharisees and almost wicked in its
rapture and rebellion against all that is smug and
" nice " : a veritable harlequinade of regeneration.
It was as if the poet had said with his hero :

> A madness took me then. I felt
> I'd like to hit the world a belt.

It was the story of the conversion of a drunken
libertine poacher who told the tale in his own way
and spared you none of the details. He revealed himself in all his old coarse language—exultingly, calling
spades " spades " indeed, sometimes doubly so. It
naturalised, or nearly, the invective of Billingsgate in
the courts of the Muse, and the Muse accepted the
offering and did not blush even at the crimson—
or scarlet—adjectives. Moreover, the few faint
protests were unavailing.

And this lurid language is not inept. It is only
when one has read Mr. J. C. Squire's amusing
" rendering " of the poem in the style of Wordsworth
that one recognises the artistic worth and power of
Masefield's reckless vocabulary. He is still champion-
ing the bottom dog, showing that under all the
ignorant filth and blasphemy which is what his
surroundings have made natural to poor Saul Kane
there is a soul struggling to rise, eager to speak,
longing for release. It is an audacious but just
testimony that profane language is not the only

nor the worst way of taking God's name in vain, and that there is more hope of the Kingdom of Heaven for Saul Kane than for the Pharisee who is shocked by his " bad words " and complacent about the conditions amid which he has learned them : it is a challenge to all that mistakes respectability for righteousness and identifies the two, such as Burns could scarce have bettered, even though a sweet wooing tenderness comes into the very words of Saul as he tells how God's Everlasting Mercy, Christ, found him and held him, and changed him, and would not let him go. He is not the first Saul whom conversion has driven to ecstasy : nor the last.

Nineteen times he went to jail. Then he broke a bargain with a fellow-poacher. To put this right, they fought in a ring about Christmas time. But Saul, knowing himself in the wrong, was uneasy— not with fear, but with contempt of things as a whole :

> And looking round I felt a spite
> At all who'd come to see me fight ;
> The five and forty human faces
> Inflamed by drink and going to races,
> Faces of men who'd never been
> Merry or true or live or clean ;
> Who'd never felt the boxer's trim
> Of brain divinely knit to limb,
> Nor felt the whole live body go
> One tingling health from top to toe ;
> Nor took a punch nor given a swing,
> But just soaked deady round the ring
> Until their brains and bloods were foul
> Enough to make their throttles howl,
> While we whom Jesus died to teach
> Fought round on round, three minutes each.

False shame prevents him owning his fault. The bout is very disgusting, and the desciiption of it is in keeping. His opponent sprains his thumb, fights gamely on, and in the eighteenth round is knocked out. So Saul wins the purse and entertains the spectators according to custom at a low tavern, also described to the life. The very pages stink of punch and husks and swine ; yet thoughts of God and shame will not leave Saul Kane amid the smutty talk and drunkenness. At last

The heat and smell and drinking deep
Began to stun the gang to sleep,
Some fell downstairs to sleep on the mat,
Some snored it sodden where they sat.
Dick Twot had lost a tooth and wept,
But all the drunken others slept.
Jane slept beside me in the chair,
And I got up : I wanted air.

I opened window wide and leaned
Out of that pigstye of the fiend
And felt a cool wind go like grace
About the sleeping market-place.
The clock struck three, and sweetly, slowly,
The bells chimed Holy, Holy, Holy ;
And in a second's pause there fell
The cold note of the chapel bell,
And then a cock crew, flapping wings,
And summat made me think of things.
How long those ticking clocks had gone
From church and chapel, on and on,
Ticking the time out, ticking slow
To men and girls who'd come and go,
And how they ticked in belfry dark
When half the town was bishop's park,
And how they'd ring a chime full tilt
The night after the church was built,

And how that night was Lambert's Feast,
The night I'd fought and been a beast.
And how a change had come. And then
I thought, "You tick to different men."

What with the fight and what with drinking
And being awake alone there thinking,
My mind began to carp and tetter,
"If this life's all, the beasts are better."
And then I thought, "I wish I'd seen
The many towns this town has been;
I wish I knew if they'd a-got
A kind of summat we've a-not,
If them as built the church so fair
Were half the chaps folk say they were;
For they'd the skill to draw their plan,
And skill's a joy to any man;
And they'd the strength, not skill alone,
To build it beautiful in stone;
And strength and skill together thus
O, they were happier men than us."

An impenitent loathing of it all asserts itself
within him. He wonders what will be his end. He
knows that he will not reform or change. He has
chosen his road, and he can't. A thought of suicide
occurs to him. But no! he "hasn't lived yet"
—he will "have his go first."

A madness took me then. I felt
I'd like to hit the world a belt.
I felt that I could fly through air,
A screaming star with blazing hair,
A rushing comet, crackling, numbing
The folk with fear of judgment coming,
A 'Lijah in a fiery car
Coming to tell folk what they are.

"That's what I'll do," I shouted loud,
"I'll tell this sanctimonious crowd

This town of window peeping, prying,
Maligning, peering, hunting, lying,
Male and female human blots
Who would, but daren't, be whores and sots,
That they're so steeped in petty vice
That they're less excellent than lice,
That they're so soaked in petty virtue
That touching one of them will dirt you,
Dirt you with the stain of mean
Cheating trade and going between,
Pinching, starving, scraping, hoarding,
Spying through the chinks of boarding
To see if Sue, the prentice lean,
Dares to touch the margarine.
Fawning, cringing, oiling boots,
Raging in the crowd's pursuits,
Flinging stones at all the Stephens,
Standing firm with all the evens,
Making hell for all the odd,
All the lonely ones of God,
Those poor lonely ones who find
Dogs more mild than humankind.
" For dogs," I said, " are nobles born
To most of you, you cockled corn.
I've known dogs to leave their dinner,
Nosing a kind heart in a sinner.
Poor old Crafty wagged his tail
The day I first came home from jail,
When all my folk, so primly clad,
Glowered black and thought me mad,
And muttered how they'd been respected,
While I was what they'd all expected
(I've thought of that old dog for years,
And of how near I come to tears).

But you, you minds of bread and cheese,
Are less divine than that dog's fleas,
You suck blood from kindly friends,
And kill them when it serves your ends
Double traitors, double black,
Stabbing only in the back,

Stabbing with the knives you borrow
From the friends who bring to sorrow
You stab all that's true and strong,
Truth and strength you say are wrong,
Meek and mild, and sweet and creeping,
Repeating, canting, cadging, peeping,
That's the art and that's the life
To win a man his neighbour's wife.
All that's good and all that's true,
You kill that, so I'll kill you."

At that I tore my clothes in shreds
And hurled them on the window leads ;
I flung my boots through both the winders
And knocked the glass to little flinders ;
The punch-bowl and the tumblers followed,
And then I seized the lamps and holloed,
And down the stairs, and tore back bolts,
As mad as twenty blooded colts ;
And out into the street I pass,
As mad as two-year-olds at grass,
A naked madman waving grand
A blazing lamp in either hand.
I yelled like twenty drunken sailors,
" The devil's come among the tailors."
A blaze of fire behind me streamed
And then I clashed the lamps and screamed,
" I'm Satan, newly come from hell."
And then I spied the fire-bell.

I've been a ringer, so I know
How best to make a big bell go.
So on to bell-rope swift I swoop,
And stick my one foot in the loop
And wave a down-swig till I groan,
" Awake, you swine, you devil's own."

He rouses the town and, half-clad, discourses at
large of hell and Sodom and Gomorrah, and tells
the lieges what he thinks of them for hypocrites

" who would, but daren't, be whores and sots,"
and when threats begin, he challenges the mob to
do its worst but first to catch him : and then runs
for it, the crowd after him. Then follows one of
Masefield's most glorious miracles.

> The men who don't know to the root
> The joy of being swift of foot,
> Have never known divine and fresh
> The glory of the gift of flesh,
> Nor felt the feet exult, nor gone
> Along a dim road, on and on,
> Knowing again the bursting glows
> The mating hare in April knows,
> Who tingles to the pads with mirth
> At being the swiftest thing on earth.
> O, if you want to know delight,
> Run naked in an autumn night,
> And laugh, as I laughed then, to find
> A running rabble drop behind,
> And whang, on every door you pass,
> Two copper nozzles, tipped with brass,
> And doubly whang at every turning,
> And yell, " All hell's let loose, and burning."
>
> I beat my brass and shouted fire
> At doors of parson, lawyer, squire,
> At all three doors I threshed and slammed
> And yelled aloud that they were damned.
> I clodded squire's glass with turves
> Because he spring-gunned his preserves.
> Through parson's glass my nozzle swishes
> Because he stood for loaves and fishes,
> But parson's glass I spared a tittle.
> He gave me a orange once when little,
> And he who gives a child a treat
> Makes joy-bells ring in Heaven's street,
> And he who gives a child a home
> Builds palaces in Kingdom come,
> And she who gives a baby birth
> Brings Saviour Christ again to earth,

> For life is joy, and mind is fruit,
> And body's precious earth and root,
> But lawyer's glass—well, never mind,
> The old Adam's strong in me, I find.
> God pardon man, and may God's Son
> Forgive the evil things I've done.

He escapes ; creeps back to the tavern ; sleeps off his debauch. Next day, he drinks again to drown his thoughts and remorse—and this time he has a royal time of it, assaulting squires, arguing with parsons, giving children oranges, and getting abuse from their scandalised mothers. But at every turn compunction rises within him. As he says, things

> made me see
> The harm I done by being me.

The only remedy is more drink, more drink. This time he stays till closing hour, and in bravado talks with defiant jocularity to a Quaker lady who visits the place on rescue work. She speaks kindly but searchingly to him of Christ.

> " Saul Kane," she said, " when next you drink,
> Do me the gentleness to think
> That every drop of drink accursed
> Makes Christ within you die of thirst,
> That every dirty word you say
> Is one more flint upon His way,
> Another thorn about His head,
> Another mock by where He tread,
> Another nail, another cross,
> All that you are is that Christ's loss."

Out in the street, he knows that change is afoot. He is aware of " some one waiting to come in."

A hand upon the door latch gropen
Knocking the man inside to open.
I know the very words I said,
They bayed like bloodhounds in my head
" The water's going out to sea
And there's a great moon calling me ;
But there's a great sun calls the moon,
And all God's hills will carol soon
For joy and glory and delight
Of someone coming home to-night. . . ."

I did not think, I did not strive,
The deep peace burned my me alive ;
The bolted door had broken in,
I knew that I had done with sin.
I knew that Christ had given me birth
To brother all the souls on earth,
And every bird and every beast
Should share the crumbs broke at the feast.

O glory of the lighted mind,
How dead I'd been, how dumb, how blind.
The station brook, to my new eyes,
Was babbling out of Paradise,
The waters rushing from the rain
Were singing Christ has risen again.
I thought all earthly creatures knelt
From rapture of the joy I felt.
The narrow station-wall's brick ledge,
The wild hop withering in the hedge,
The lights in huntsman's upper storey
Were parts of an eternal glory,
Were God's eternal garden flowers,
I stood in bliss at this for hours.

And as he goes about the sweet country he sees a
ploughman at his work and he thinks how Christ
is " ploughman of the sinner's soul . . . to plough
the living man from sleep." More than that, he

feels God asks the aid also of every man "to help
Him plough a perfect line."

> I kneeled there in the muddy fallow,
> I knew that Christ was there with Callow,
> That Christ was standing there with me,
> That Christ had taught me what to be,
> That I should plough, and as I ploughed
> My Saviour Christ would sing aloud,
> And as I drove the clods apart
> Christ would be ploughing in my heart,
> Through rest-harrow and bitter roots,
> Through all my bad life's rotten fruits.
>
> O Christ who holds the open gate,
> O Christ who drives the furrow straight,
> O Christ, the plough, O Christ, the laughter
> Of holy white birds flying after,
> Lo, all my heart's field red and torn,
> And Thou wilt bring the young green corn,
> The young green corn divinely springing,
> The young green corn forever singing;
> And when the field is fresh and fair
> Thy blessèd feet shall glitter there,
> And we will walk the weeded field,
> And tell the golden harvest's yield,
> The corn that makes the holy bread
> By which the soul of man is fed,
> The holy bread, the food unpriced,
> Thy everlasting mercy, Christ.

He begins an honest life in Farmer Callow's service.

This lengthy abstract of *The Everlasting Mercy*
may seem anything but critical; may seem also to
destroy the balance of this primer, since the same
treatment cannot within reasonable space be accorded
to all its successors. Yet it must be conceded that
as the central event (so far) in Mr. Masefield's literary
career, this extraordinary poem (which at once

thrilled the whole world) has an importance that
warrants our giving it conspicuous place. There is
more stately, more artistic, and even more passionate
work in later volumes—but in this is the primal
surge of new life ; a new wellspring in English verse,
not yet quite clear of soil maybe, but stimulant
and athrill with the fire of its origin and first upheaval ;
a torrent of inspiration. From being told in *oratio
recta*, it has qualities of speed and vigour no other
tale by Masefield has caught. The mystery of all
imagination and imaginative work is in it, causing
us to wonder how the like of this could ever be
imagined, and we are sure that the poem—whether
it be now and again reminiscent of something
autobiographical or not—is a complete analogue
of what has happened to the artist as artist :
though it is passing strange to think of Mr.
Masefield's delicate imitation verse in *Ballads* and
the prose peccadilloes of *A Tarpaulin Muster* in
terms of the unregenerate Kane's exploits ! Indeed,
even yet, there are readers " of the old school " who
would find it even more shocking to liken the reckless
audacity of the new poem to the regeneration of
its central figure. But, whatever its faults, it is
abrim with life, new life and more abundant, where
the earlier verse was but beauteous as the white
poppies laid upon the breast of a dead queen.

No doubt *The Everlasting Mercy* has been enjoyed
by many for bad reasons—not for base reasons, as
a rule, but for reasons irrelevant to art. Many
minds—worlds removed from the very thought of
pruriency—are excited by any frank allusion to, or
mention of, such startling facts as are flung broadcast
by Saul Kane ; and the large virtue that lies in even
the most petulant futile and youthful open assault

upon such things has an interest even for those whose experience, stolidity and self-control regard the outcry itself with contempt, or with but kindly passing pity as the outcome of the cruel vision granted to youth only to be withdrawn or forgotten by and by. Interest so created and maintained is legitimate enough, but it has little to do with the goodness or badness of a work of art. This strong and passionate verse has many flaws in common with other poems by Mr. Masefield shortly to be mentioned, but it has some virtues unshared by any. Even *Reynard the Fox*—perhaps only because of the lesser exaltation of theme—has not the great burst of vital force that impels this. Here of all places we know that Mr. Masefield is a man indeed before he is poet or aught else. Here his strength of personality reveals itself with a flame that scorches up the attention we would bestow on the weaknesses of verse .and rime. Rhythm, intensity, reality—the three tests for great poetry of to-day—are here beyond a doubt. The great theme has been more greatly sung in other days. But for our little day this is the best expression it has had, and the revelation is authentic and original.

VII

FOOD FOR PARODY

The Everlasting Mercy was almost immediately followed by *The Widow in the Bye Street*. Mr. Harold Monro—whose rather hastily and casually written *Some Contemporary Poets* (1920) may do for the Georgian age what Mr. William Archer's weightier *Poets of the Younger Generation* (alas ! for the swift years) did for us of the Edwardian interlude—considers it the best of Masefield's narratives : and Mr. Monro's opinion on poetry is entitled to respect, in spite of the dislike engendered by the frank and rather fierce judgments he metes to his fellows. Nevertheless, it is the one of all the poems which to me seems to call for distinctly unfavourable judgment, not forgetting even *The Daffodil Fields,* although none can gainsay its interest as a yet new unhackneyed note in our poetic literature. Masefield was still " hitting the world a belt " in it, and the world was needing that—as the world indeed always *is*. But it has to be done in a new way each time.

The poem of *The Widow* is constructed upon a much less exalted story ; a sordid affair ending in sorrow for all and the gallows for the widow's son, Jimmy Gurney, beguiled by an infamous woman whose paramour he killed in frenzy. Of course, Masefield's point is the victory of love in the sad heart of the old wrecked widowed mother, who loses her reason—but it is a squalid police-court tale of

lust, brutality and crime. True, no doubt: and
not without a measure of interpretation of such
horrible facts in human life as well as a didactic
influence; but far too scantily meditated, too
hurriedly turned out, to do justice by such interpretation or to discover to others the indubitable
beauty to be found even in such scenes and minds
as it hales before our eyes and nostrils. The widow's
memories of her laddie's babyhood and the almost-
inconsequence of the last conversation between
Jimmy and his mother in the condemned cell are
both truth and pathos at white heat; and we
can't have *that* without the very essential beauty.
Regarded aright, the most beautiful pitiful lines in
English poetry might easily be Lear's

> Never, never, never, never, never!

or

> O Desdemona! Desdemona! dead!
> Oh! Oh! Oh!

But the poet must needs have fathomed and funda-
mentally touched the emotion responsive to these.
The prison interview in *The Widow in the Bye Street*
does so. But who could at once be sure that Mr.
J. C. Squire, parodist, had not played the trick on
Mr. Masefield's manuscript which the friends of the
sporting parson alluded to some pages back played
on his Bible, when one finds this in the court scene:

> Guilty. Thumbs down. No hope. The judge
>   passed sentence:
> " A frantic passionate youth, unfit for life,
> A fitting time afforded for repentance,
> 'Twas certain justice with a pitiless knife.
> For her his wretched victim's widowed wife,
> Pity. For her who bore him, pity. (Cheers.)
> The jury were exempt for seven years."

It was natural, perhaps, that *The Everlasting Mercy* should come all in a fiery burst, but no poet can go on " throwing off " spiritual masterpieces, and much of Mr. Masefield's work at this time suggests hurry, carelessness, and at times even slovenliness. Now, Art can give no quarter to any of these things nor admit them unto her kingdom. That Mr. Masefield should have published four long poems like these in two years was itself a warning.

It may be hazardous to assume that the order of their publication gives any sort of evidence as to the order of these poems' composition. But more than mere fancy or personal predilection suggests that *The Widow in the Bye Street* was written in the inevitable season of exhaustion after so tremendous a spending of vital force as *The Everlasting Mercy*, however spontaneously originating, must have cost. Its raggedness hints of a weary artist and a flagging musical sense and imagination ; its frequent dullness proclaims the weaker work of a time of recuperation. In the same way, *Dauber*, published third of the series and in many respects a very great poem even as it is unique among pæans of the sea, was followed by *The Daffodil Fields*—a story hardly nobler than *The Widow* in theme, and betraying reaction and lapses into sentimentality and self-parody everywhere. Every individual work of Mr. Masefield's has some characteristic unshared by all the others. *The Daffodil Fields* has the unhappy distinction of being his one poem crammed with conventional counters. Adjectives of purely conventional usage and value bristle in it. It has charming pages of tender natural description, but one feels that much of it has been turned out like machine-made

furniture ; that the poet is allowing his invention,
his new inspiration, to run to seed. The theme is
not perhaps so revolting as that of *The Widow*.
The loves of two men and one woman and the hard
fortune Fate dealt them make the plot, and in the
end the two men slay each other through anger
just when their wayward lot has made it more
possible to solve the cruel tangle and save some
poor threads of their three wasted passion-riven lives.
The scene, changing from England to the Argentine
and back to England again the while, is always
captured in all the loveliness of its natural beauty,
and every now and again we are lifted out of a great
patch of tedious incongruous prose into a zenith of
song, and Love now and again sings with a full pure
tone, and the final tragedy is not ignoble though
slightly reminiscent and therefore dangerously apt
to suggest parody. The book has charm, if read
almost as one reads an ephemeral magazine idyll
to while away a railway journey. It is worthy of
being read to better advantage than that. It is a
good melodrama, although, told thus in narrative verse,
it is apt to drag. There is point in the flippancy
of a Glasgow reviewer who remarked that twelve
currants and three raisins hardly make a plum-
pudding. It is a question whether it might not
have made as fine a drama as *Nan* ; but the poet
judged that it would not. In this form the story is
nearly intolerably slow, with some three or four
intensely moving passages where passion soars into
unmistakable poetry. Even these, however, suffer
from their context inasmuch as it gives them the
appearance of having been interpolated to brighten
things up : as if the poet had even said (as his clever
parodist playfully makes him in effect say), " Go

to ! it is now time to impart a tender touch, to become inspired." How a poet who can carry you for three hundred lines close to heaven's gate can endure without a qualm so to drag his story through long, arid stretches of desert beats me.

No poet of such merit has so lacked the salutary ruthlessness of merciless self-criticism. The meticulous patience of Horace or Pope is a gift which unfortunately (on the whole) the fairies left not at his cradle. It is not so easily understood—not so readily set down to carelessness and unconscious lack of humour—when one looks back at the finicking perfection of the early imitative verse. Yet one is persuaded that it is not a deliberate feature of the revolt, not a mere scorn of technical precision and power. It may be due to over-hasty production and premature publication ; but certainly one result is a whole host of faults of a most ludicrous sort which have marred a great proportion of Mr. Masefield's work and which bid fair to deprive it of the immortality and endurance that much of it merits if he will not take an artist's pains to overcome them and cast them out. Even though they figure less frequently and less glaringly in his more recent volumes, they are by no means absent, and it is only fair to his work that we should mark these amazing motes and try to account for the accident.

Sometimes it is a fault of taste—the coarseness is overdone. It is intended to make for verisimilitude, but it doesn't—it is a parody of even the vilest life of slumdom. The poet, deprecating the snobbery of banning the bottom dog from Art, is a little guilty of another snobbery in quite needlessly talking down to the bottom dog and for him, and in making him out more absurd in general than he ever is in reality.

That is to say in other words that while nothing
in human life is unfit for Art, this sort of thing—
as *selected* and isolated by Masefield, at all events—
has nothing to do with human life : and when you
have curses " neatly measured through a stanza "
the effect is most ludicrous.

Again, there are lapses into the sheerest, baldest
prose—so flagrant sometimes that one wonders if
the poet has any design in dropping thus ruinously
to the banality of commonplace—and the trick of
breaking suddenly into an artificially tender passage
of nature-description, or moral emotion and plati-
tudinous sentiment only emphasises this, and itself
becomes a rather silly and ineffective mannerism.
The Widow is replete with it.

> So tea was made, and down they sat to drink ;
> O the pale beauty sitting at the board !
> There is more death in women than we think,
> There is much danger in the soul adored.
> The white hands bring the poison and the cord ;
> Death has a lodge in lips as red as cherries,
> Death has a mansion in the yew-tree berries.

These patches frequently make one feel that it
doesn't matter what (if anything) in the world they
mean. When the story is resumed—

> There's that purple passage done,
> And I have one less lap to run !

The padding, too, is notorious. Whole chunks
seem to exist simply because the rime must be met
or the measure filled out. This occurs in *Rosas*.
It is part of a letter :

> If I go naked hence, you know the cause.
> I keep my father's name. When I am gone
> I shall be gone for ever. *I am, John.*

The italics (we may quote) are ours. They are
hardly necessary. Masefield errs outrageously at
times in this respect.

Then his evil rimes are innumerable, incredible,
not to be explained by any toleration of, or preference
for, assonance such as a Celt might plead : " floor
dust " with "sawdust," " lie sweet " with " High
Street," " banner " with " bandanna," " bastard "
with " lasted," " bowler " with " Hispaniola,"
" thought " with " report," " Susans " with " nuisance," " border " with " marauder," " corner " with
" yawner," " floor " with " O Lor ! ", " bearers "
with " *Sierras*," and many another loose irresolute
pair. It is not merely that a Scottish ear over-
values the " r's." Nothing so painfully shows how
superficial was the delicacy cultivated in the
early imitative verses as their failure to educate
the ear beyond the possibility of falling into such
atrocities.

It is not necessarily a flaw that Mr. Masefield
invariably gives that royal word " fire " the value
of a dissyllable, but what is to be said of the metrical
grace of a line like

> A rotten liar who inspires lies ?

And even allowing for the stress theory whereby
much loveliness of music and colour has in our day
been liberated from bondage, it is difficult to pass
such instances as

> After triumphant hours quickening hearts,

and

> A resonant wire-hum from every rope,

and

> Two hours passed, then a dim lightening came.

In subject-matter, too, the poet does sometimes seem to go out of his way to dilate upon the horrible and the unclean. Now, as one critic has pointed out, Shakespeare wrote *King Lear* and Shelley *The Sensitive Plant,* and Dante too, like them, achieves much gorgeous unpleasantness. But their treatment makes poetry of it. Can it be said of Mr. Masefield that *he* shares their achievement? On the whole, No. He has not the artistic restraint; and the riot which rang true with fire and inspiration in *The Everlasting Mercy* simply cannot be repeated. In spite of the anecdotes in *St. George and the Dragon,* I am inclined to agree that Mr. Masefield's greatest lack is the lack of humour. *The Street of To-day* has already suggested it. A keen sense of humour would surely save him from many a sad fall into rubbishy utterance in this regard; prevent the strange mixture of poetry and wood. Even his galleries of swear-words, as Mr. Robert Lynd has said first, somehow lack zest. They impress one with neither horror nor pagan relish. He seems to be regarding them all the while with such sad, serious eyes, and shaking his head in melancholy. They strike one as being awfully, painfully innocent for swear-words. It may be due to his great pity, his earnest brotherliness for all humble lives—but we compare him with J. M. Barrie, and we say, " Another little twinkle wouldn't do him any harm." The profanity is apt to be merely crude, and after *The Everlasting Mercy* it somehow seems jaded and faded, no longer original or inspired. It becomes a question of how much of that sort of prose a poem can stand without ceasing to be a poem, and Masefield risks too much with this guilelessness and his perilous disregard of his tendency to self-parody.

Yet how great in essence must this poet and his
work be when in spite of these vast and most un-
poetical faults it still charms, is still redeemed ! It is
the token of good verse that it can suffer deliberate
parody and yet survive, and no poet has been so
unmercifully parodied as this of ours. Yet even
after Mr. Squire has made us yell with amusement
or writhe with the pain of its suppression, we turn
to Masefield's work and find it potent still. Mr.
Squire has been apt in his capture of the Masefield
manner (whose manner has he not deftly, impishly
captured ?), and no doubt with all these mannerisms
it lends itself well to his naughty art ; and, to a nature
bubbling with fun, *The Widow in the Bye Street,*
with its horrors told in such simple-Simonwise,
would prove an irresistible temptation. Accordingly,
Mr. Squire tells of a similar widow quite in the
Masefieldian vein :

> She had twelve children (quite a lot)
> And often wished that she had not .
> Among her seven strapping sons
> Were several interesting ones :
> Even the Baby James for instance
> Had killed a man without assistance :
> And several more, in divers ways,
> Had striven to sing their Maker's praise.
>
> .   .   .   .
>
> Hedda Lucrezia Esther Waters,
> The eldest of the widow's daughters,
> In early infancy absorbèd
> A dreadful liking for the morbid.
> She much preferred the works of Ibsen
> To those of Mr. Dana Gibson,
> And when she went to bed at night
> She prayed by yellow candle-light :
> " Six angels for my bed,

> Three at foot and three at head,
> Beardsley, Strauss, Augustus John,
> Bless the bed that I lie on.
> Nietzsche, Maeterlinck, Matisse,
> Fold my sleep in holy peace."

His tale of Flo, the Barmaid who murdered an impertinent customer, and was converted by the Salvation Army and then " done in " by the mother she was no longer able to support, is, in fitting parlance, a scream! But his version of *Casabianca* " as Masefield would have written it " (in *Tricks of the Trade*) is the cleverest delineation imaginable of all the mannerisms and a pleasant form of criticism to boot.

> " You dirty dog," " You snouty snipe,"
> " You lump of muck," " You bag of tripe,"
> Such, as their latest breaths they drew,
> The objurgations of the crew.
> —— —— —— they roared
> As they went tumbling overboard,
> Or frizzled like so many suppers.
> All along the halyard scuppers.
> " You ——" . . . the last was gone
> And Cassy yelled there all alone,
> (He thought the old man was on the ship,)
> " Father! this gives me the fair pip!" . . .
>
> Dogs barked, owls hooted, cockerels crew,
> As in my works they often do
> When, flagging with my main design,
> I pad with a descriptive line.
> Young Cassy cried again : " Oh, damn!
> What an unhappy put I am!
> Will nobody go out and search
> For dad, who's left me in the lurch ?
> For dad, who's left me on the poop,
> For dad, who's left me in the soup,

For dad, who's left me on the deck.
Perhaps it's what I should expeck
Considerin' 'ow he treated me
Before I came away to sea."

Often at home he used to beat
My head for talking in the street,
Often for things I didden do,
He brushed my breeches with a shoe.
O! how I wish that I was home now,
Treading the soft old Breton loam now,
In that old Breton country where
Mellows the golden autumn air,
And all the tender champaign fills
With hyacinths and daffodils,
And on God's azure upland now
They plough the ploughed fields with a plough,
And earth-worms feel averse from laughter,
With hungry white birds following after.
And maids at evening walk with men
Through the meadows and up the glen
To hear the old sweet tale again.

Enough by way of sample! It requires some effort
like Margaret Ogilvy's against the insidious R. L. S.
to refrain from transferring one's allegiance holus-
bolus to Mr. Squire. His view infects the dullest
sufficiently to see a new aptness in Masefield's

> I clodded Squire's glass with turves
> Because he spring-gunned his preserves.

But Mr. Squire has not caught in these parodies
(so far as I have detected) the graphic musical
imaginativeness with which his model frequently
evokes genuine mysteriousness.

> They had a death look, wild and odd,
> Of something dark foretold by God.

And Mr. Squire himself in his own serious poems
has once or twice echoed Mr. Masefield unmistak-
ably—a just recompense, surely.

> In vain pursuit of glittering things,
> In fruitless searching, shouting, running,
> And greedy lies and candour cunning

(something of romantic Milton here, perhaps : but
this is unmistakable—

> And shows the bells and all their ringing,
> And all the crowds and all their singing, . . .)

This apart, it is the best of testimonies to Masefield's
poems that we still can read them feeling that their
greatness can't be laughed away, and that—in spite
of all—he has revealed high possibilities even in
doggerel (the bottom dog, that is, of literature),
the democracy of words. He is true to his early
Consecration, even among things verbal.

VIII

SONNETS AND SHORTER POEMS

ABOUT a decade ago there appeared in a Christmas number of *Chambers's Journal*, under the title of *Four Hundred Years Ago*, a most affecting and beautifully wrought imaginative account of the coming of the fatal news of Flodden Field to Scotland's archiepiscopal and university town of St. Andrews —still a haunted town, as Andrew Lang has it,

> Though shrunken from thine ancient pride
> And lonely by thy lonely sea.

The writer was Mr. R. L. Mackie, a Scottish historian of rare imaginative and literary gift.[1] That idyll, never republished so far as I can find, comes vividly to recollection as often as I lift Mr. Masefield's *Philip the King*, in which—a few years later, and in verse—he has rendered the like tragedy in Spanish history with much of the same fantasy and with nearly as much of the desolation and sorrow of battle-defeat as makes the more ancient and simpler of the two *Flowers of the Forest* melodies so emotionally unbearable in any land.[2]

[1] R. L. Mackie : *Robert the Bruce* (Harrap, 1913), *History of Scotland* (Harrap, 1916), *Social and Industrial History of Britain for Schools* (Harrap, 1921).

[2]
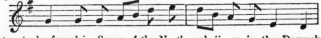

etc., to be found in *Songs of the North*, vol. ii., or in the Dawyck

It is hardly a drama. It is much more nearly
a conversation, a monologue, a vision, a pageant, a
reverie ; an epic compressed into a long lyric, a
High Requiem of Dead Warriors. It is one of the
noblest expressions of refined patriotism in our
literature ; and, along with one or two other pieces
in the same volume—*The Wanderer, Ships, Biography*
—it stands at the head of all the verse-literature
of the glory of ships. I say " verse literature,"
remembering our poet's deathless telling of deathless
Gallipoli. *Dauber* is, of course, less a poem of ships
than of the sea.

Philip the King is primarily an imaginative
recounting of the defeat of the Great Armada by
act of God and of the tidings borne home of disaster.
Over all broods a melancholy of forlorn grandeur,
an atmosphere heavy with imaginative significance
and association gathered from the emotions of
bygone histories,

> a sorrowful loveliness
> Out of the battles of old times.

The *Song of Roland* echoes in the very opening :

> All night long it talked to me
> Of a trouble there is beyond the sea.
> A trouble of war . . . I heard a horn
> Blowing forlorn,
> And I knew that it came from far away,
> From men of Spain in a pass at bay.
> Blowing for help ; the beaten call
> None heeds at all.

The poem is full and final proof that Mr. Masefield

Edition of Scottish Song, by Arthur Somervell (Boosey & Co.),
and some other collections, but usually displaced by the more
conventional, modern and sophisticated setting.

has kept more of the grace of his early writing than
his longer narrative poems would suggest, that
stateliness and majesty are well and permanently
within his power after all, and that on occasion he
can build verse of great musical and spiritual exaltation. Nay, the whole piece has that magic that
communicates itself with a thrill of a " grand surmise "
to passages which out of their context are devoid
of one distinguished word,

> Ship after ship is running down the Bay
> With news,

and that puts the whole of pathos in the fall of a
commonplace couplet.

> PHILIP.   The hand of God will bring us through the deep.
> PRINCESS.   Amen, my father, but my heart is breaking.

The description of the great fleet by the Princess
is ablaze with the strength of ships and a beauty
with which even the Crispin Crispian speech in
Henry V is no more than comparable with all its
magnifical rhetoric.

> I was conscious then
> That I beheld the greatest fleet that men
> Ever sent seaward.

And even the tedious reiteration of the adjective
" lovely " throughout the poem is little remarked,
as the heart dilates with the throes of chivalry
distrest. Before King Philip, fulfilled of devotion
and fatefulness as he abides the hazard, passes
vision of Indian slaves brushed and despoiled by
Spanish colonising ; heretics butchered by the fiery
devildoms of the Inquisition ; his murdered bastard

brother, Don John, who won him Lepanto and
could have won him England now had not cruel
jealousy and suspicion laid him low; Santa Cruz,
the builder of the Fleet even now deflowered,
reproaching:

> Why did you give away my splendid sword,
> Forged by a never-conquered captain's brain,
> Into the hoof-hand of an ambling lord,
> Useless in all things, but to ruin Spain?
> Would God I had but guessed it! Would my stars
> Had shown me clearer what my death would bring,
> I would have burned those galleons, guns and spars,
> Soldiers and all, and so have stopped this thing.
> And doing that I should have served you well . . .

and last of all, De Leyva:

> come
> Out of the sea, my everlasting home
> To whisper comfort to my ruined friend.

While the air is sullen and heavy with bodings of
destiny, an English prisoner is brought with news
or conjecture of victory, and all yield to joyance,
to odes of triumph, shouts of ecstasy, adoring grati-
tude to Heaven and solemn ritual silences; though
still in the brain of the King lurks a dim persisting
ominous dread:

> I thought I heard, far off, a funeral call;
> As in your dream, a melancholy cry.

And sure enough, upon the hilarity and festal
banners and chanted lauds come Recalde's shattered
remnant and the Black Monks in penitential psalm:

> Defeat's not victory, but 'tis bought as dear.

.   .   .   .   .

MESSENGER.

This gold chain . . .
Bears the twelve badges of the strength of Spain
Once linked in glory, Philip, but now loosed.
(*Detaching link from link.*)
Castilla, Leon, Aragon, and these,
Palestine, Portugal, the Sicilies,
Navarre, Granada, the Valencian State,
The Indies, East and West, the Archducate,
The Western Mainland in the Ocean Sea.
Those who upheld their strength have ceased to be.

It is a pity that the record does not end the poem
in a high sorrow of loss. Mr. Masefield is truer to
history—the history that repeats itself—than to art
in insisting repeatedly and unnecessarily on allowing
Philip to interject his cold, complacent one-line
sayings about Fate, the will and wisdom and support
of God, misfortune bringing no stain, *et hoc genus
omne*, upon speech after speech built up of broken
Glory's beauty and crying hearts on lips writhen
with calamity ; intruding on narrative that towers
to a veritable worthy agony of lyric lamentation.

But when all is said, this—with *August 1914* in
the same volume—is one of the very few poems of
war which stood the fierce test of reality so soon
and cruelly to be imposed on hearts and song alike.
There is nothing in it, of which after the floods of
wrath and woe have abated, and jingoism has blown
its worst and evaporated, we need be ashamed
or by which we are disgraced, if we read this pre-war
poem as the ballad and anthem of our own broken
souls to-day, and if, as we contrast the hapless
doom of Spain and Philip with our own salvation
and deliverance, we are reproved lest we forget.

At least five other poems add notably to the
dignified splendour of this book : perhaps the one

book of verse by Mr. Masefield delivered from even
a breath or vestige of anti-climax; a fit com-
panion for *Gallipoli* and *The Faithful*. These are
The Wanderer, *Ships*, and *Biography*, already com-
mented on; *August 1914*, his one deliberate poem
of the Great War, and one of the finest elegies ever
wrought; and *The River*, a piece of cruel realism
with a sturdy moral gospel in its core and a
terrifying image at its close. Really, one can never
quite understand why the long narratives should
enjoy a wider fame and popularity than these things
of perfect strength and gallant loveliness and truth.
Like their ships, "they are grander things than all
the art of towns"; and largely for the same reasons.
They are the true laureate songs of England and
her "Beauty in hardest action, beauty indeed."

> I touch my country's mind, I come to grips
> With half her purpose thinking of these ships.

Of all Mr. Masefield's books *Lollingdon Downs* is
the hardest to apprehend. It contains seventy
lyrical pieces, mostly sonnets. Occasionally one
thinks that a gleam of sequence has visited one
from these, but almost immediately it has vanished.
There are short-line songs like the slighter things
in the *Philip* volume, a somewhat school-bookish
colloquy between the components of a ship from the
ore upwards, a folk-song lilt that makes one think
pleasantly of the days of sedan-chairs till it suddenly
proves to be quite exceedingly modern, a passage
in dialogue-verse that might have come from a
discarded version of *Pompey*. The eighth lyric is
a beautiful piece of decorative panelling, and a
confessio fidei of an artist to boot; *Midnight*, the
twentieth, a fragmentary anticipation of *Reynard*

the Fox; its two neighbours are like early derivatives of Kipling, Yeats and A. E. Housman. One poem, unhappily, mars the sheaf—an amazing grotesque.

Young Will, the son
Heard his sister shriek ;
He took a gun
Quick as a streak.

He said : " Now, Dad,
Stop, once for all ! "
He was a good lad,
Good at kicking the ball.

His father clubbed
The girl on the head.
Young Will upped
And shot him dead.

" Now, sister," said Will,
" I've a-killed father,
As I said I'd kill.
O my love, I'd rather

A-kill him again
Than see you suffer.
O my little Jane,
Kiss good-bye to your brother."

It surely is impossible that verses discarded from the earliest collections as second-rate and experiments of the groping transition period which had been left aside as unsuccessful were brought to light when fame and popularity had opened a market for them (I do not mean by this to make the sordid suggestion of a *commercial* market). Some unpublished work has a way of charming strangely after it has thus been laid aside for a while, just as some in print after a like period has lost all suggestion of charm :

but it is impossible to account for the serious production in public of *this* item. Nevertheless it is
ungracious, rather than impartial, to quote these
weak versicles while leaving unquoted " Night is
on the downland," or " The Kings go by with
jewelled crowns," or " I went into the fields."

As to the sonnets—grouped in varying quantities
throughout the book, but according to no plan that
I can trace—one must confess to some puzzlement.
They are certainly suffused by pensivity and feeling,
lit by a faintly glowing music—but vague : vague as
these efforts to describe them. They are all about
Beauty—not beauty, more is the pity—and, for
all their wondering grace, they make nothing about
it definite. Even while one is haunted by the sense
—or the shadow—of something elusive and vanishing
as we follow the flying feet, the suspicion that such
indefiniteness must surely be a symptom of the
febrile and the false will not leave us. It is not the
fiery, stringent, haughty Beauty. It has no comely
arrogance. It rarely has the magistral brow. It
lacks the Platonic μανία. The symbols evoke nothing.
Melody murmurs like a hidden brook, but the sound
of the waters is low. There is something autumnal,
nearly decadent, about them. Now they seem
boyish and old as the songs of adolescent
heartache ; anon they are whispering through
images of awe the agony of world-war raging
while they grow. They appear to be informed
with a dreamy theosophy—thin, unsubstantial
phantoms caught in blind hands stretched out
in dark night to grasp a vaster science, a deeper
undiscovered law in things, than all man's knowledge
yet has brought mankind. Immortality, immortal
Beauty, unity of all things formed and uncreate,

hither, O hither!—but (wakening up) what *is* it
all about ? Oriental cults of mystery may know
the secret, and it is notable that the poems included
in this volume not as quite new were first published
in America, where the study of comparative religion
—or at least curiosity about beliefs other than
Christian—and the quest of the arcane and occult
and ultimate has devotees more numerous than here.

But the trouble lies not in that. Nothing could
be more subtle than the presentation of an obscure
neo-Platonic doctrine, for instance, such as we have
in Rachel Annand Taylor's marvellously coloured
word-picture of *Ecstasy* : [1]

> O ye that look on Ecstasy
>   The Dancer lone and white,
> Cover your charmèd eyes, for she
>   Is Death's own acolyte.
> She dances on the moonstone floors
> Against the jewelled peacock doors :
> The roses flame in her gold hair,
> The tired sad lids are overfair.
> All ye that look on Ecstasy
>   The Dancer lone and white,
> Cover your dreaming eyes, lest she—
> (*Oh, softly, strangely !*—) float you through
> These doors all bronze and green and blue
>   Into the Bourg of Night.

—but all there is perfectly definite. The tantalised
reader of the *Lollingdon Downs* sonnets (and even
of those in the *Enslaved* volume) sometimes has a
fear that Mr. Masefield himself knows hardly better
than he what is attempted in them ; and Art abhors
the blurred and the vague from all eternity. The
occult and the vague—even mere ghosts of emotional
ideas, the faintest stirrings in the Unconscious itself,

[1] *Rose and Vine* (Elkin Mathews, 1909), p. 134.

the unformed psychic fears—may be fit subjects for
artistic treatment; but the treatment itself may
not lawfully be vague, and we are not convinced
that it is altogether the reader's fault when these
verses refuse to give up their secret or to say if they
have any secret to declare or to retain, though there
is far more than enough glamour discernible in them
to make us feel stupid at failing to recognise what
they seek. The facile Shakespearean form is but
doubtfully a benefit to their desired object.

> You are too beautiful for mortal eyes,
> You the divine unapprehended soul;
> The red worm in the marrow of the wise
> Stirs as you pass, but never sees you whole.
> Even as the watcher in the midnight tower
> Knows from a change in heaven an unseen star,
> So from your beauty, so from the summer flower,
> So from the light, one guesses what you are.
> So in the darkness does the traveller come
> To some lit chink, through which he cannot see,
> More than a light, nor hear, more than a hum,
> Of the great hall where kings in council be.
> So, in the grave, the red and mouthless worm
> Knows of the soul that held his body firm.

" Exactly," we should like to say. . . . And yet,
complaint is ill-befitting this book, too. It baffles
and annoys a considerable company of Mr. Masefield's
younger admirers—those who have patience, but
only a little, for what lies deeper than the obvious
delights and glories of verse. Nine out of ten will
almost certainly let slip a parenthetic opinion that
" *Lollingdon Downs* isn't up to his usual standard ";
and even with a guilty conscience, oneself will
almost as invariably retort with a savour of heat,
" It is his profoundest work, and about his best."

It may be that so we speak more truly than we
dream ; and it is startling and significant that of
the many sincere young spirits who have gone back
to the Sonnets as humble seekers on hearing this
retort from a critic whom they believe they have
reason to respect, quite half have returned to confess
that they had indeed been mistaken in their casual
estimate. Ourselves, we have struggled with some
of these poems alone and in company, brooded and
dreamed over them and carried them into the day's
tasks with us—always with a sense of repayment
and deepened appreciation even of what remains
elusive in them. Hasty judgments are suspended or
recalled. " Aye, this is gey good," we say : and
we *are* Scots, it may be admitted ; but give us
accuracy, accuracy always.

Enslaved and Other Poems (1920) may be considered
in this chapter mainly because, like the two volumes
already dealt with, it is made up of shorter poems—
Animula, a brief sonnet-sequence strangely like (and
as strangely unlike) Meredith's *Modern Love* ; other
sonnets, like that *On Growing Old*, with a right brave
ring and a fine artistic firmness.

> Men are no gods ; we tread the city dirt,
> But in our souls we can be queens and kings

it is written in *Forget*. There are two eerie ballads
of some length also—*Cap on Head*, a verse-version
of the tale *In a Castle Ruin* previously written in
A Mainsail Haul ; and *The Hounds of Hell*, another
treatment of the supernatural which is full of terror
and exhilaration—the " medievalesque " story of a
saint who fought with the powers of darkness,—and

no mean performance from any point of view. But
the leading poem, for all its pathetic story, disappoints.
Even the story is quite incredible—not that that
matters much, but that it is lack of art that accounts
for the failure of illusion—and the pretty music
has more than a twinge of self-parody. Owen
Hanrahan in *The Secret Rose* " under a bush of may "
called down his comprehensive curses on all things
but its blossom—" Because it comes in beauty, and
in beauty blows away "—in this rhythm, and we
rather liked it there ; but here it is apt rather to
recall " The people who write in secret what in
public they allege to be folk-songs " of *Tricks of
the Trade.*

The suggestion already made to account for the
crudities of *The Widow in the Bye Street* and
The Daffodil Fields may apply in a measure
here. This book appeared between the issue of
Reynard the Fox (1919) and *Right Royal* (1920),
and if *The Everlasting Mercy* and *Dauber* induced
lassitude and exhaustion by their triumph and
ascendancy, so might the yet more perfect if jollier
fox-hunt poem, which even to *read* is to ache with
its vulpine hero. Anyhow, *Enslaved* is soft and
sentimental, and we are not sure that of the poet's
two extremes we do not prefer the outrageous.
The exigencies of rime are once more too great for
a writer evidently in as desperate a hurry as his
fugitives :

> " This key, that should unlock, is sticking : try."
> With shaking hands I took the clicket, I.

But even so, the cadence and detail of the canto
describing the slaves' cavern in the Moorish night
is a superb example of Masefield at his best. This

is the minute, live kind of thing he always does
supremely well :

Then as the tide came in, the water seething
Under the quarries, mingled with the breathing,
Until the prison in the rock y-hewen
Seemed like a ship that trod the water's ruin,
Trampling the toppling sea, while water creeping
Splashed from the seams in darkness on men sleeping.
Far in the city all the dogs were howling
At that white bird the moon in heaven owling.
Out in the guard-house soldiers made a dither
About the wiry titter of a zither,
Their long-drawn songs were timed with clapping hands

     .   .   .   .   .

The water hissed its life out on the sands,
The wheel of heaven with all her glittering turned,
The city window-lights no longer burned.
Then one by one the soldiers left their clatter ;
The moon arose and walked upon the water,
The sleepers turned to screen her from their eyes.
A fishing-boat sailed past ; the fishers' cries
Rang in the darkness of the bay without.
Her sail flapped as she creaked and stood about,
Then eased, then leaned, then strained and stood away.
Deep silence followed, save where breathers lay.

IX

THE SENSE AND SPIRIT OF ENGLAND: *DAUBER—REYNARD THE FOX—RIGHT ROYAL—KING COLE*

FOUR more long narrative poems—two of them certainly great and enduring poems—remain for comment. We can give them little more. These, of all his works, must assuredly be read.

Dauber was given to us in 1913 by *The English Review,* which had already printed *The Everlasting Mercy* and *The Widow in the Bye Street.* I think it was the publication of *Dauber* that overcame all doubts that lingered as to the genuineness of Mr. Masefield's poetic impulse or as to his power of sustained effort. None questioned henceforth that a new poet had arisen and that he had " come to stay."

Dauber is a young painter. His impulse and call and longing is to paint the sea; and he must do it from experience, not from convention. A poor, slight lad and rather finely strung, he goes to sea as a sailor before the mast and, in his leisure time, studies and sketches and paints. He is a jest to all the crew, the crew being English (or British, as Scotsmen sometimes prefer to say). Some brutal, but not malicious, tricksters destroy all his work with turpentine and wellnigh break his heart. But he proves himself a man, and before the voyage ends, while rounding the Horn, there is such a storm as no other English poem knows, and in the crisis poor little Dauber, who has passed through his spiritual baptism of impassioned and painful experience in the travesty befalling his cherished work, is first at the masthead in the terrific endeavours to save the ship. And first down—for he falls to the deck and breaks his spine, and dies with his genius in him, unused. But he has achieved himself, his manhood—and so " saved his soul "; and *that* robs death of bitterness, and his faith is that nothing shall be lost, that there is no call to sentimentalise over " untimely " death.

> He said, " It will go on,"
> Not knowing his meaning rightly, but he spoke
> With the intenseness of a fading soul
> Whose share of Nature's fire returns to smoke
> Whose hand on Nature's wheel loses control.
> The eager faces glowered red like coal.
> They glowed, the great storm glowed, the sails, the mast.
> " It will go on," he cried aloud, and passed.

With all its faults—and there are the usual ones —*Dauber* is a great poem; great because of its pictures of the storm, the sea night, the ship entering the calm bay at day-dawn. But great also as a book of revelation; as a book of intense, terrible, pitiful heroic vision; as a sensitive record of the sea, full of the bright face of danger, the endurance of ships, the endurance of men.[1]

It is a spiritual vision of life, a soul's confession, an acceptance of life on life's terms, essentially Christian, tragic in its joy. And it is instinct with life. It is the work of " a man who writes of what he has experienced, not of what he thinks he can imagine : who has braved the storm, who has walked

[1] Some of these epithets are Mr. Robert Lynd's (*Old and New Masters*).

in its hells, who has seen the reality of life and does
not attempt to imagine shipwrecks from the sofa.
Compare *Enoch Arden* with *Dauber*. One is a
beautiful dream ; the other is life " (Charles H.
Sorley). Mr. Masefield has realised the heart's
desire of his hero :

> It's not been done, the sea, not yet been done,
> From the inside, by one who really knows ;
> I'd give up all if I could be the one.

Whether it has been done in Dauber's art, I know
not ; but Sir Edward Elgar has done it in music,
Mr. Conrad in supreme prose, and Mr. Masefield as
supremely (one would hazard) in verse. Swinburne
knew the sea well, but only in a few of its moods.
He would have felt a deep generous joy in the younger
poet's unrivalled sea-pictures ; as Robert Bridges
—one would not say Doctor Shelley—who created
A Passer-By, undoubtedly does. It is quite impossible
for our generation to believe that they are not
immortal as the sea itself and British love for it.
It was indeed a thing most proud

> To share man's tragic toil and paint it true,

and if nobler or more romantic realism in verse
than fills the dozen opening stanzas of Canto VI
exists I have had the singular ill-fortune not to
meet with it. Criticism, one feels, can do nothing
for such work, and our lingering over it is utterly
of wonder, delight, of praise and thanks to Heaven
that our eyes have seen it and our ears heard.

> I love all beauteous things,
> I seek and adore them ;
> God hath no better praise
> And man in his hasty days
> Is honoured for them.

By a consensus of opinion, by far the firmest and best knit of Masefield's poems is *Reynard the Fox*, published late in 1919, the year of the beginnings of Peace in Europe, the year of many a foul reaction but a time also of rejuvenation, uplift and love of the dearly-delivered land, such as no century knows twice. It is a splendid poem. There is scarcely a single dragging line in it : not a flaccid tissue in the whole. It is away, away from the grime and slime and crime of back streets, and except for a few quite needless coarse remarks and a very rare lapse into commonplace it breathes the pure air of the glorious countryside it describes. It is a glorification of England—its holy, lovely fields and soil, its jolly love of sport—and this was ever a wish of Masefield's, as it was of Robert Burns's, to sing his country's self. How he revelled in the perfect poetry of English country life found in the Gloucester-shire scenes of *The Second Part of King Henry IV* :

The kindness and the charm of the country servants, so beautiful after the drunken townsmen, are like the English country speaking. The earth of England is a good earth and bears good fruit, even the apple of man. These scenes are like an apple-loft in some old barn, where the apples of last year lie sweet in the straw.

And yet, while still praising Shakespeare, he justly remarks that

It is a strange and sad thing that the English poets have cared little for England ; or, caring for England, have had little sense of the spirit of the English. Many of our poets have written botanical verses, and braggart verses ; many more have described faithfully the appearance of parts of the land at different seasons. Only two or three show the mettle of their pasture in such a way that he who reads them can be sure that the indefinable soul of England has given their words something sacred and of the land. Shakespeare attained to all the spiritual powers of the English. He made a map of the English character. We have not yet passed the frontiers of it. It is one of his humanities that the English country, which made him, always meant much to him, so that, now, wherever his works go, something of the soul of that country goes too, to comfort exiles over the sea. Man roams the world, wandering and working; but he is not enough removed from the beasts to escape the prick in the heart that turns the tired horse homeward, and sets the old fox padding through the woods to die near the earth where he was whelped.

Is not this *confessio amantis* a truer diagnosis of the undoubted nostalgia in Masefield's English poems than that of Mr. J. Middleton Murry—that princely critic—who fears that we have in it the hint of a deeper-seated decadence which, while adding to the power of the poem to appeal to the consciousness of its own age, will deprive it of enduring charm for later days, being of "its time" untimely? It is a controversy which only time can settle. There will be reactions from Masefield as there have been from Pope or from Tennyson; and, as in these cases, there will be counter-reactions. He has not the heart-whole naturalness of Chaucer, to be sure, as Mr. Murry shows.[1] But it is not certain that Shakespeare himself had, if nostalgia mars it or removes.

Even conceding a point to Mr. Murry, we doubt if the occasional trace of nerves rather than of true nerve in this poem justifies for a moment the verdict that it is "tainted by the desperate *bergerie* of the Georgian era!" or the conviction that thus imperfectly is *ended* the stage of Mr. Masefield's poetry in praise of England.

[1] J. Middleton Murry : *Aspects of Literature* (Collins, 1920), p. 153.

Certainly the landscapes are deftly, minutely brought to the eye in a phrase. Mr. Murry contends that virtually every feature is over-emphasised as if Masefield did not, and could not afford to, trust the associative appeal of the features themselves ; as if the nostalgia amounted to a " consciousness of separation," an alienship occasioning such an uncertainty and overstrain as needs to be (and cannot be) compensated for by an overloading of every rift with ore, and by shovelling even the *mud* of England into his lines to the detriment and destruction of its fragrance and glory. The crowds and the huntsmen are delineated with telling strokes of character such as English poetry has hardly known since Chaucer's *Prologue*, and each one stands out distinct—yet Mr. Murry's delicate sense (and the author of *Cinnamon and Angelica* has few peers in delicacy) detects here also blemishes of artifice, marks and affectations of the outsider and pretender, in epithets such as appear in

> Under his hide his heart was raw
> With joy and pity of these things,

and the flaw cannot be gainsaid, though the generalisation may. We hope—and we think that the wish is not father to the thought in this contention—that these marks of fever and " conscious inquisition " do not constitute so debilitating a presence of reaction as Mr. Murry's exposition claims. For evidence to the contrary we point to the humour —real humour, for once—that surrounds and follows in the hunt. Even Mr. Squire admits (in the *London Mercury*) that Mr. Masefield " has pulled it off with *Reynard*."

The second half of the poem is the hunt proper

—and not a doubt of it, whatever be the extent of the faults referred to, you run, feel, ache with the fox and almost sob with relief at his escape. The baffled hounds catch and rend another fox, it is true ; but thank goodness ! not ours, not Masefield's.

Against Mr. Murry's quotations we might (no more arbitrarily) set these and urge that the self-conscious streak, the parody of England, is discernible here in so infinitesimal a degree that it almost savours of pessimism to count the poem damned of durability because in yonder corner the streak is drawn a little thicker.

The parson was a manly one,
His jolly eyes were bright with fun.
His jolly mouth was well inclined
To cry aloud his jolly mind
To every one, in jolly terms.
He did not talk of churchyard worms,
But of our privilege as dust
To box a lively bout with lust
Ere going to heaven to rejoice.
He loved the sound of his own voice,
His talk was like a charge of horse,
His build was all compact, for force,
Well-knit, well-made, well-coloured, eager.
He kept no Lent to make him meagre,
He loved his God, himself and man,
He never said, " Life's wretched span :
This wicked world," in any sermon.
This body that we feed the worm on,
To him, was jovial stuff that thrilled.
He liked to see the foxes killed ;
But most he felt himself in clover
To hear, " Hen left, hare right, cock over,"
At woodside, when the leaves are brown.
Some grey cathedral in a town
Where drowsy bells toll out the time
To shaven closes sweet with lime,

And wallflower roots rive out the mortar
All summer on the Norman dortar
Was certain some day to be his;
Nor would a mitre go amiss
To him, because he governed well.
His voice was like the tenor bell
When services were said and sung,
And he had read in many a tongue,
Arabic, Hebrew, Spanish, Greek.

So much for portraiture. As for narrative: at times in the fox's race for life our attention is first riveted, and then suddenly we are imaginatively so inside the shaggy, taggled coat that we forget the poetry and all in the tense pain that possesses us —and if illusion and compassion be any test of power in narrative verse, Chaucer himself could not better the passage beginning

And here, as he ran to the huntsman's yelling,
The fox first felt that the pace was telling;

and ending less than fifty lines later (can that be all?) with this:

Within as he reached that soft green turf,
The wind blowing lonely, moaned like surf,
Desolate ramparts rose up steep
On either side, for the ghosts to keep.
He raced the trench, past the rabbit warren,
Close-grown with moss which the rain made barren;
He passed the spring where the rushes spread,
And there in the stones was his earth ahead.
One last short burst upon failing feet—
There life lay waiting, so sweet, so sweet,
Rest in a darkness, balm for aches.

   .   .   .   .   .

The earth was stopped. It was barred with stakes.

As if to continue his pæan of English sports and open air, Mr. Masefield within a year followed this vigorous poem of the hunt with a steeplechase tale in verse, *Right Royal*.

It has no plot. Charles Cottrill, who is riding his own Right Royal in a Cup 'chase, has a dream of victory (which he believes the horse has shared) and stakes his all on him, now that he has been retrained by love, in spite of his bad past record. This is the confession made to his sweetheart, Emmy Crowthorne, for whom, of course, marriage and home and all have been jeopardised by this mad gamble. Mr. J. C. Squire will not allow that this poem repeats the achievement of *Reynard the Fox*. Certainly, the course is narrower; the descriptions less clearly focused; there are a few—only a few —dips into prose; the tendency to self-parody reappears—though we do not detect it in the description of Emmy, as Mr. Squire does; being blinded, perhaps, by the memory of these lovers (or one of them) in the earlier poem :

> He looked to men like young Delight
> Gone courting April maidenhood,
> That has the primrose in her blood

Metaphysical agents too (quite properly introduced in *The Dynasts*) are dragged in somewhat absurdly towards the end of the race : with which they perceptibly interfere. But this apart, the verse goes swiftly, and once again we concentrate all our attention on Royal. If we are not constrained to this so masterfully as in *Reynard*, we are none the less wellnigh breathless from start to finish—" Is he to win ? " is our one concern as the 'chase proceeds : and that says much for a narrative poem. There is a huge field. We go twice round the course. There are thirty horses and twenty-eight jumps. There are numerous accidents. At one hurdle Royal falls and, recovering, is thirty lengths behind. But there is a perfect unity of spirit possible between man and nature, man and brute, and it is achieved to-day between Royal and his master. Charles cannot hurry the horse, and will not. Towards the end, when he is one of the six or seven possible victors, the others use lash and spur, but not he. Royal " knows best himself." It is his Day. At the perfect instant he makes his effort, as it were spontaneously, and in a desperate finish wins by half a length.

Speed and vividness are like light in the verse, as Sir Lopez, the favourite, and Right Royal fly side by side with their riders towards the post:

Right Royal went past him, half an inch, half a head,
Half a neck, he was leading, for an instant he led ;
Then a hooped black and coral flew up like a shot,
With a lightning-like effort from little Gavotte.

The little bright mare, made of nerves and steel springs,
Shot level beside him, shot ahead as with wings.
Charles felt his horse quicken, felt the desperate beat
Of the blood in his body from his knees to his feet.

Three terrible strides brought him up to the mare,
Then they rushed to wild shouting through a whirl of blown
    air ;
Then Gavotte died to nothing ; Soyland came once again
Till his muzzle just reached to the knot on his rein.

Then a whirl of urged horses thundered up, whipped and
    blown,
Soyland, Peterkinooks, and Red Ember the roan.
For an instant they challenged, then they drooped and were
    done ;
Then the white post shot backwards, Right Royal had won.

The life of the sea in storm, the fox-hunt, the steeplechase—what other theme is equally redolent

of England now that Mr. Squire has given us a
vivid football poem ? [1] There is the travelling circus.
And in *King Cole* (1921) Mr. Masefield has turned his
attention thither, sketching with quick sympathy
the woes of an itinerant showman and his artist-
comrades, who are led to fame and fortune and royal
favour by the influence of the central figure, the
Spirit of that good King Cole from whom old Chelsea
derives its name, who is permitted still by the Acquit-
ting Judges of Heaven for the goodness of his earthly
rule to wander benignly abroad to succour mankind
—half "scholar gipsy," half "pied piper." It is
not so sensational a poem as its predecessor, not
so impetuous ; but it has a quiet glamour all its
own. It is more austerely knit, and its stanzas are
free from the conventional adjectives that mar
The Daffodil Fields, which it resembles in measure.
Occasionally a couplet will savour of pad and
jingle still, and, although more rarely than ever,
the verse will sometimes drop to a jejune platitude.

> "Yes," said his wife. "Thank God, we still are able
> To help a friend ; come in, and sit to table."

> THE WIFE. I think that traveller was an angel sent.
> THE SHOWMAN. A most strange man, I wonder what he
> meant.

or

> KING COLE. . . . The life of man is stronger than good
> taste.
> THE PRINCE. Custom is stronger than the life of man.
> KING COLE. Custom is but a way that life began.

Intentionally or not, the events of the tale are
apt to pass too suddenly. When the Prince and

[1] "The Rugger Match" : *London Mercury*, 1921.

all his Court are on their way to the deserted circus
tent and King Cole, disguised as courier, brings in
the plump bags of minted gold

> He gave a sack that she could scarcely hold.
> She dropped it trembling, muttering thanks, and then
> She cried : " O master, I must tell the men " ;

and when the lost son is restored to the showman
and his wife—it all happens in so many most matter-
of-fact words.   Not that the words should be effusive
—but there lacks that " pause," that emotional
quality, that allows the pathos of a simple statement
or deeply charged speech to have its due effect.
And as a climax

> The audience, standing, sang " God Save the Queen."
> The hour of the showman's life had been,

is decidedly bad.

But the virtues of the poem quite outshine all
the trifling flaws.   It has the atmosphere of the
show, with a streak of fancy banners and fairy-town
twilight over it, and it has a happy ending.   Ever
so many lines of pictorial power startle and thrill
one, and even the passages cataloguing flowers and
butterflies are pleasant and fantastic.   The humani-
tarian poet again shows his compassion for all sorts
and conditions of men—the worn-out impatient
troupe, the broken showman, the Prince so far from
free that he covets the lot of a cat.

> Wearily plodding up the hill they went
> Broken by bitter weather and the luck,
> Six vans, and one long waggon with the tent,
> And piebald horses following in the muck,
> Dragging their tired hooves out with a suck,
> And heaving on, like some defeated tribe
> Bound for Despair with Death upon their kibe .

Yet all of that small troupe in misery stuck
Were there by virtue of their nature's choosing
To be themselves and take the season's luck,
Counting the being artists worth the bruising.
To be themselves, as artists, even if losing
Wealth, comfort, health, in doing as they chose,
Alone of all life's ways brought peace to those.

It is the very metre of Wordsworth's *Resolution and Independence*, by the way—one of the few Wordsworthian poems that Mr. Masefield finds tolerable, strangely enough—and many a stanza might deceive a chance reader into thinking he had lighted on that mighty poet. But the stanza gives place to the couplet at times.

" It puts a crown of lead upon my brain
To live this life of princes," thought the Prince
" To be a king is to be like a quince,
Bitter himself, yet flavour to the rest. . . .
The man who plaits straw crowns upon a rick
Is happier in his crown than I the King.
And yet, this day, a very marvellous thing
Came by me as I walked the chamber here
Once in my childhood, in my seventh year,
I saw them come, and now they have returned,
Those strangers, riding upon cars that burned
Or seemed to burn, with gold, while music thrilled,
Their beauty following till my heart was filled
And life seemed peopled from eternity.
. . . those strangers from I know not where,
From glittering lands, from unknown cities far
Beyond the sea-plunge of the evening star,
Would give me life, which princedom cannot give.
They would be revelation . . ."

But if this poem enhances the author's reputation, it will be simply because he shares something of the musical and imaginative grace of his own hero and has the power to convey "atmosphere." It is not distinguished rimes or subtle new discoveries in cadence or rhythm that give him his appeal. But just as the draggled strolling circus is glorified by the Spirit of King Cole before men's eyes and recalls the tired Prince to his childhood years, so for most men there is an atmosphere as of a lost townlet, seen once long since in a strange light of evening, the memory or half-memory of which some music and some verse—and many another thing—has power to evoke, troubling them with the pensivity of associations now far beyond recall, if ever they were actual : and it is vain to hope to convince the one affected that the mystery and the power does not lie in the agent of that dim delightful evocation, or that it fails as Art or is lacking in beauty when it has fired him with that glow. Thus : when *King Cole* brings back the glamour, and makes one think of Thrums or Ludlow or St. Andrews, or Goldsmith's Auburn or "the days of the Kerry dancing," or me of a summer evening when I was five years old and saw a glimmer on all things in the nowadays dull town of Alyth—is it not perchance wisest to believe that indeed some such spirit does haunt places and the works of men, even as the poet tells, and that his own verse is irradiate by it ? Mr. Yeats— probably indirectly — gave me that idea long ago, and the genius of locality has become more real ever since ; it needs but to be touched or named, and it lives. Therefore, although I think it beautiful, I cannot be sure whether it is his conscious art or the spell of a real Cole on his page that makes me rejoice in Mr. Masefield's latest poem.

And when the planets glow as dusk begins
He pipes a wooden flute to music old.
Men hear him on the downs, in lonely inns,
In valley woods, or up the Chiltern wold ;
His piping feeds the starved and warms the cold,
It gives the beaten courage ; to the lost
It brings back faith. . . .

Then at a window looking on the street
He played his flute like leaves or snowflakes falling,
Till men and women, passing, thought, " How sweet ;
These notes are in our hearts like flowers falling."
And then, they thought, " An unknown voice is calling
Like April calling to the seed in earth ;
Madness is quickening deadness into birth."

And through the town the liquid piping's gladness
Thrilled on its way, rejoicing all who heard,
To thrust aside their dulness or their sadness
And follow blithely as the fluting stirred
They hurried to the guild like horses spurred.
There in the road they mustered to await,
They knew not what, a dream, a joy, a fate.

And man to man in exultation cried :
" Something has come to make us young again."

The close of this kindly poem contains two lines
as fine as any in Mr, Masefield's work.

Out of the living world of Christendom
He dimmed like mist till one could scarcely note
The robin nestling to his old grey coat,

Dimmer he grew, yet still a glimmering stayed
Like light on cobwebs, but it dimmed and died.
Then there was nought but moonlight in the glade,
Moonlight and water and an owl that cried.
Far overhead a rush of birds' wings sighed,
From migrants going south until the spring,
The night seemed fanned by an immortal wing.

X

GALLIPOLI AND WAR WORKS

No social enthusiasm throbs so passionately, so indignantly, in Mr. Masefield's work as the loathing of war between nations, hatred of its foulness and iniquity and inevitable futility, disdain for the reckless or selfish sophistries that justify preparation for (or against) it, the cowardice that from afar accepts it as defensive, the romantic lying that affects to see a shred of glory in the thing itself. There are moral equivalents for it, as is indeed spiritually needful, and there is a reading (but no facile reading) of so-called non-resistance that gives ultimate and incontrovertible right to those who profess and practise that. The violation of personality implied by its actual details, the actual details themselves, and the idea that it may have a judicial function in God's economy (Mozley's way of expressing, and veiling, the doctrine that might is right) impel horror, revolt, a lonely antagonism of such a destiny, a readiness (were there a need *and* a chance) to go down scornful under many spears: or, it may be, not scornful, but in expiatory and substitutionary love.

This, as has been seen, is part of the problem of Mr. Masefield's Pompey. It is spoken passionately in *The Faithful. Multitude and Solitude,* and the more directly political *Street of To-day,* show how it surged in protest in the growing idealist souls of the early twentieth century. Stabs of what was to be nicknamed Pacifism in the time as yet hidden are very frequent in these books.

"If that is the case," said the Major triumphantly, "it proves my point. If we are likely to go to war, we ought to be prepared for war. And we can only be prepared if we establish conscription. And if we are not prepared we shall cease as a nation. It is your duty, as an English writer, to awaken the national conscience by a play or a novel, so that when the time comes we may be prepared."

"My duty is nothing of the kind," said Roger. "I believe wars to be a wasteful curse; and the preparation for war to be an even greater curse, and infinitely more wasteful. I am not a patriot, remember. My State is mind. The human mind. I owe allegiance to that first. I am not going to set Time's clock back by preaching war. . . . You think that that is decadence. That I am a weak, spiritless, little-Englander, who will be swept away by the first 'still, strong man' who comes along with 'a mailed fist.' Very well. I have no doubt that brute force can and will sweep away most things not brutal like itself. It may sweep me away. But I will not disgrace my century by preaching the methods of Palæolithic man. If you want war, go out and fight waste. I suppose that two hundred and fifty million pounds are flung away each year on drink and armaments in this country alone. I suppose that in the same time about five hundred pounds are spent on researches into the causes of disease. About the same amount is given away to reward intellectual labours. I mean labours not connected with the improvement of beer or dynamite. Such labours as noble imaginings about the world and life. . . . You send women to prison for wanting to control such folly. If I am to become a propagandist, I will do so in the cause of liberty or knowledge . . . but for a military man, who merely wants food for powder, for no grand, creative principle, I would not write even if the Nicaraguans were battering St. Paul's."

It was, and is still, easy to speak pleasantly of the Nicaraguans! *Litera scripta manet.* The whole

passage is interesting alike as literature and as
politics, and may be studied in *Multitude and Solitude*. The eruption of war from Germany in August
1914 showed all of us how many elements our discus-
sions, our theories, had overlooked, how much our
idealism had not adequately confronted. The
confusion of our plight was by and by made plain.
Those who clung to the faith behind the quotation
just made certainly raised a question in Christian
ethics which has not yet been faced, and yet must
be, will we, nill we. On the other hand, they found
—and are the readiest and most sorely humbled in
owning it—no nobler, harder alternative, not even
a glorious failure, in the networks of circumstance
which entangled minds and affections and passions
then, and bound us hand and foot in more ways
than one.

It would be vain in an essay like this to diverge
further along these lines from our examination of
Mr. Masefield's writing in its own qualities. But
such a course of thought is not pursued without
passion, nor without passion surrendered or post-
poned : and the inimitable book on *Gallipoli* can
breed admiration the better when we know that
this lies behind it. Whatever it cost him, the man
who imagined Roger Naldrett and his views, was
wholeheartedly a patriot in the day of Britain's
ordeal by battle. One cannot picture him a jingo.
Nothing is more honourable in him—nothing more
eloquent of his sanity and scrupulousness as an
artist—than the fact that his war-poetry consists of
only one poem, and that one the brave, sad elegy
August 1914, quiet with sober pity and with courage.
One can very easily fancy him aloof and disdainful
of success, turning from the boast and braggart

insolence of Britain in her pride. But Britain with
her back to the wall, Britain in the smoking trenches
dying—*that* was, is, and ever shall be, a different
concern : a country, a city of the soul, whose calamity
even among the things of sense no righteous man
of all her sons would care to, or consent to, survive.
And that was the jeopardied chivalrous Britain
that her poet saw, that commanded still the most
convinced pacifist not less (but far more) than the
flag-flapping, money-grubbing mobs that swarmed
against him. And that was the Britain whose
deathless dying on the Peninsula by the Ægean
Mr. Masefield has told so majestically in an art not
elsewhere his. *Gallipoli* is a book to strike the
critical faculty numb and hush the heart of the
hearer. For an age—aye, for ever on the earth so
far as we can dream it—it will be read and gloried
in afresh and heads will be bowed and the tears of
strong men nobly shed at every telling. It is as
yet too sacred for applause. The truest criticism of
its art—and it is criticism, even as the other is Art,
still—is to quote : and cry, Behold !

In fine weather in Mudros a haze of beauty comes upon
the hills and water till their loveliness is unearthly, it is so
rare. Then the bay is like a blue jewel, and the hills lose
their savagery, and glow and are gentle, and the sun comes
up from Troy, and the peaks of Samothrace change colour,
and all the marvellous ships in the harbour are transfigured.
The land of Lemnos was beautiful with flowers at that season,
in the brief Ægean spring, and to seawards always, in the
bay, were the ships, more ships, perhaps, than any port of
modern times has known ; they seemed like half the ships
of the world. In this crowd of shipping strange beautiful
Greek vessels passed, under rigs of old time, with sheep and
goats and fish for sale, and the tugs of the Thames and
Mersey met again the ships they had towed of old, bearing

a new freight, of human courage. The transports (all painted black) lay in tiers, well within the harbour, the men-of-war nearer Mudros and the entrance. Now in all that city of ships, so busy with passing picket-boats, and noisy with the labour of men, the getting of the anchors began. Ship after ship, crammed with soldiers, moved slowly out of the harbour in the lovely day, and felt again the heave of the sea. No such gathering of fine ships has ever been seen upon this earth, and the beauty and the exultation of the youth upon them made them like sacred things as they moved away. All the thousands of men aboard them gathered on deck to see, till each rail was thronged. These men had come from all parts of the British world, from Africa, Australia, Canada, India, the Mother Country, New Zealand, and remote islands in the sea. They had said good-bye to home that they might offer their lives in the cause we stand for. In a few hours at most, as they well knew, perhaps a tenth of them would have looked their last on the sun, and be a part of foreign earth or dumb things that the tides push. Many of them would have disappeared for ever from the knowledge of man, blotted from the book of life none would know how—by a fall or chance shot in the darkness, in the blast of a shell, or alone, like a hurt beast, in some scrub or gully, far from comrades and the English speech and the English singing. And perhaps a third of them would be mangled, blinded or broken, lamed, made imbecile or disfigured, with the colour and the taste of life taken from them, so that they would never more move with comrades nor exult in the sun. And those not taken thus would be under the ground, sweating in the trench, carrying sandbags up the sap, dodging death and danger, without rest or food or drink, in the blazing sun or the frost of the Gallipoli night, till death seemed relaxation and a wound a luxury. But as they moved out these things were but the end they asked, the reward they had come for, the unseen cross upon the breast. All that they felt was a gladness of exultation that their young courage was to be used. They went like kings in a pageant to the imminent death.

·   ·   ·   ·   ·

When the darkness cleared they were still there, line after line of dots, still more, still moving forward and halting and withering away, and others coming, and halting and withering away, and others following, as though these lines were not flesh and blood and breaking nerve, but some tide of the sea coming in waves that fell yet advanced, that broke a little farther, and gained some yard in breaking, and were then followed, and slowly grew, that halted and seemed to wither, and then gathered and went on, till night covered those moving dots, and the great slope was nothing but a blackness spangled with the flashes of awful fire.

What can be said of that advance ? . . . It was their thirteenth day of continual battle, and who will ever write the story of even one half-hour of that thirteenth day ? Who will ever know one-hundredth part of the deeds of heroism done in them, by platoons and sections and private soldiers, who offered their lives without a thought to help some other part of the line, who went out to cut wire, or brought up water and ammunition, or cheered on some bleeding remnant of a regiment, halting on that hill of death, and kept their faces to the shrapnel and the never-ceasing pelt of bullets as long as they had strength to go and light to see ?

.   .   .   .   .

There was the hour for a casting off of self, and a setting aside of every pain and longing and sweet affection, a giving up of all that makes a man to do something which makes a race, and a going forward to death resolvedly to help out their brothers high up above in the shell bursts and the blazing gorse. Surely all through the 8th of August our unseen dead were on that field, blowing the horn of Roland, the unheard, unheeded horn, the horn of heroes in the dolorous pass, asking for the little that heroes ask, but asking in vain. If ever the great of England cried from beyond death to the living they cried then. *De ço qui calt. Demuret i unt trop.*

.   .   .   .   .

To us the taking of Sari Bair meant the closing of that road to the passing of Turk reinforcements and the opening of the Narrows to the fleet. It meant victory, and the beginning of the end of this great war, with home and leisure for life again, and all that peace means. Knowing this, our soldiers made a great struggle for Sari Bair, but Fate turned the lot against them. Sari was not to be an English hill, though the flowers on her sides will grow out of English dust for ever. Those who lie there thought, as they fell, that over their bodies our race would pass to victory. It may be that their spirits linger there at this moment, waiting for the English bugles and the English singing, and the sound of the English ships passing up the Hellespont.

Sari was not to be our hill. Our men fought for four days and nights in a wilderness of gorse and precipice to make her ours. They fought in a blazing sun, without rest, with little food and with almost no water, on hills on fire and on crags rotting to the tread. They went, like all their brothers in that Peninsula, on a forlorn hope, and by bloody pain they won the image and the taste of victory ; and then, when their reeling bodies had burst the bars, so that our race might pass through, there were none to pass, the door was open, but there were none to go through it to triumph. And then, slowly, as strength failed, the door was shut again, the bars were forged again, victory was hidden again, all was to do again, and our brave men were but the fewer and the bitterer for all their bloody sacrifice for the land they served.

.   .   .   .   .

It was said by Dr. Johnson that " no man does anything, consciously for the last time, without a feeling of sadness." No man of all that force passed down those trenches, the scenes of so much misery and pain and joy and valour and devoted brotherhood, without a deep feeling of sadness. Even those who had been loudest in their joy at going were sad. Many there did not want to go, but felt that it was better to stay, and that then, with another 50,000 men, the task could be done, and their bodies and their blood buy victory for us. This was the feeling even at Suvla, where the men were shaken and sick still from the storm ; but at Anzac, the friendly little kindly city, which had been won at such cost in the ever-glorious charge of the 25th, and held since with such pain, and built with such sweat and toil and anguish, in thirst, and weakness, and bodily suffering, which had seen the thousands of the 13th Division land in the dark and hide, and had seen them fall in with the others to go to Chunuk, and had known all the hope and fervour, all the glorious resolve, and all the bitterness and disappointment of the unhelped attempt, the feeling

was far deeper. Officers and men went up and down the
well-known gullies moved almost to tears by the thought
that the next day those narrow acres so hardly won and all
those graves of our people so long defended would be in
Turk hands.

What they had done will become a glory for ever, wherever
the deeds of heroic unhelped men are honoured and pitied
and understood.

Turning to the Western theatre of war, Mr. Masefield later published *The Old Front Line* and *The
Battle of the Somme* (*Fricourt-Pozières*). The former
deals minutely with the whole British line of battle
prior to the advance begun on July 1, 1916—an
advance so costly, so chequered, so slow ; ground
literally gained by yards, and lost and gained again,
and nearly lost irretrievably and—as if by miracle
(miracle it was !)—taken at last, gripped, tugged
from infernal jaws and held, held. But in this book
the author does not attempt to renew or repeat
the epic, the heroic song, of the *Gallipoli* ; perhaps
with more than his usual share of an artist's wisdom,
knowing that that way lay naught but parody ;
rather, perhaps, with a mourner's sense that the
time for singing, were it the loftiest, was past ; that
this was the hour of the power of darkness and
that war here and now was stripped of all illusion ;
that here was no episode of grandeur and forlorn
hope greatly faced leading to another such defeat
as should for ever be more than conquest ; that
here was the stand of and for the last stark realities
of life and love and time, and that Picardy was a
shambles, English faith at that tense place where
faltering and doubt feel their own presence, and
tears—and worse, tearless grief—and tortured hearts
and broken minds everywhere fighting out that

other battle of the natural and the spiritual order.
Very simply, very reverently, without the intrusion
of a word of pity, or of sympathy, Mr. Masefield
explained every place along the whole line from
which so many of our sons and brothers had since
gone out to the death for their native land : so that
the places can all be seen and the bereaved have a
satisfaction for which there are only a few who
crave not.

> No country know I so well
> As this landscape of hell.
> Why bring you to my pain
> These shadow'd effigys
> Of barb'd wire, riven trees,
> The corpse-strewn blasted plain ?

> And the names—Hebuterne,
> Bethune and La Bassée—
> I have nothing to learn—
> Contalmaison, Boiselle,
> And one where night and day
> My heart would pray and dwell.[1]

Remains *St. George and the Dragon*, a book of
addresses on the war delivered as propaganda in
America after her entrance to the conflict : and
here, again, as the triumph or the hope of it begins to
arise again, stayed by a new ally, there is something
of the high notes of poetry as in *Gallipoli* : largely
indeed in further and briefer reference to that cam-
paign. But this is earnest and sometimes pleasant
conversation ; anecdotage rather than literature,
than saga. Sometimes the pathetic touch is senti-
mentalised—but there, this is not a page for

---

[1] Robert Bridges, *October and other Poems*, p. 31. An English
mother, on looking into Masefield's *Old Front Line*.

criticism. It was offered not as literature, and the interests that will long make it readable and keep it alive—memories of the war, pleas for Anglo-American goodwill and co-operation for the world's peace—are not the interests directly of literature.

XI

A TEMPORARY CONCLUSION

IT is a truism that contemporaries cannot foresee the estimate that coming ages will make of any poet. It requires a rare critical detachment (in itself an impediment in other ways) to penetrate and sunder the transient and the enduring elements in his work. A writer like Stevenson is hardly ever regarded even yet except through the veil of his bodily sufferings. Yet these can affect only temporary judgments, and the quality of his work as art is quite independent of his physical weakness, except in so far as heroism evoked against it strengthened his writing. The danger of dwelling on it, as contemporaries unduly do, is that it creates a morbid interest in something that is quite apart from the literature which is all that will be of deep interest to a century that has not known the author. It is not always a gain to an author, considered as artist, to have had a picturesque personality : it detracts from his work, may even focus attention upon that in it which is less honourable and less beautiful than his best. It has probably been good for the glorifying of Shakespeare's work that so little has been known of its maker ; and among poets of whom it is not incongruous to speak in the same breath as has named Shakespeare, Robert Burns has suffered untold neglect and depreciation

10

as artist and poet because attention has been accorded
to the man and deflected from him, as often as not,
to parts of his work wholly unworthy of his mighty
gift. The case of Tennyson is trite in this connec-
tion : only now is his fame finding equilibrium after
the Victorian adulation of his good and bad alike,
and the subsequent reaction (or distortion) caused
by the younger generation's perception of its
tawdry elements, its Victorian lumber, almost to
the exclusion of the great imaginative glories it
holds.

Accordingly we judge it wise to hazard no final
opinion here as to Mr. Masefield's place and perman-
ency. Yet he stands for some new things in our
poetic literature. The sea has never been more
lovingly, more intimately sung. England's green and
pleasant land must count him one móre of her
apostles. He is a poet of democracy, of submerged
and squalid democracy, the bottom dogs of life ;
and even in the language that parallels these in the
peerage of words he has made discoveries of veins
of true and passionate poetry—for there *is* a residue
of gold fire after all the dross is consumed—and
beauty for ashes has been in his gift. He is a poet
of pity, and something nobler than pity (even justice),
for all hunted, ill-used, broken things ; for man and
beast. He has brought back activity and energy
to our days of decadence, if he has not indeed wholly
escaped the withering blight of its feverishness in
some strains of his poetry. He has also dealt with
life as it is found among men—and that was needed ;
and it would have been a good thing even that it
should be attempted without success. How much
more is it so when it has given us *Dauber* ?

It is natural to liken Masefield to Geoffrey Chaucer.

The comparison may be flattering to the modern poet. You may fear at times, with Mr. Middleton Murry, that even his love of England and the open air is too conscious ; that there lurks a subtle sickness and fever behind it, a nausea, a fear ; something decadent, calling for a subtle psychiatry, utterly unknown to the genial happy Chaucer with his humour and unforced gaiety. You, too, may wonder whether this may not be the dry-rot that shall deprive his work of durability and hide from men of the coming ages what we, at so close range and sharing unawares with it the passions and frets of our age, think we see in it. Only time—and a generation able to judge our fevers, being freed from them and able to see them plain—can tell. It may be he will not remain.

Nevertheless another possibility increasingly suggests itself to me. Happily his work, we may hope, is not yet finished ; not by much. We have seen already how Mr. Masefield achieved a delicate perfection in his early mode, and then in the fulness of time cast it from him and by-and-by gradually began to master a stronger, braver, more individual —if at first somewhat turgid—style, in which *Reynard the Fox* at least suggests that he is approaching something like perfection. He certainly surmounted triumphantly at that stage of his work the peril and crisis of which he wrote so understandingly in his *Shakespeare,* and which it has been the aim of this study, this " chronicle," to sketch with sympathy and (let us hope) insight.

He had reached a point of achievement that is always a critical point to imaginative men. He had reached the point at which the personality is exhausted. He had worked out his natural instincts, the life known to him, his pre-

dilections, his reading. . . . The personality was worn to
a husk. It may be that a very little would have kept him
on this side of the line, writing imitations of what he had
already done. He was at the critical moment which separates
the contemplative from the visionary, the good from the
excellent, the great from the supreme. All writers, according to their power, come to this point. Very few have the
power to get beyond it. . . .

And very few of the few who do are so vital as
to come again to such a crisis and successfully
o'erpass it. Soon or late, most become self-parodists
—not merely occasionally, as nearly all do, but
essentially : writing imitations of what they have
already done in the first watch, or at best, in the
second, which so few enter at all. But it is possible
—one says no more than that—that Mr. Masefield,
like his great masters, Chaucer and Shakespeare,
may in his own way have a " third period " ; that
the time may be approaching when he will as decisively
and radically pass from his second stage (into which,
out of years of mental strife and torment, he
emerged with *The Everlasting Mercy*) as he passed
from his juvenile æstheticism, and perhaps dazzle
and delight us as never man before, or as never this
man before. That is more than one dare predict.
It must depend in part on a certain freedom—from
deliberate aim at change, and from nervous self-
consciousness,—which the very knowledge of such
a possibility's existence endangers. It must be the
gift of the gods, and it will not come save to a fine
and almost inconceivable carelessness of spirit wed
to a diligent care in craft. It will not come if Mr.
Murry's tracing of a morbid neurasthenia of soul
pervading the work is a just diagnosis, as I am still
persuaded it is not. The odds are always

immensely, magnificently, against it—in every case.
But it is possible

For the Life is near change that has uttered its best.

And if our standards are true, there are more than
scattered hints of perfection—of mastery, at all
events—in *Reynard the Fox* : and in any case, not
very much more can be done in this vein, without
passing from the Power which does not suffer vain
repetitions. It may be that, like the superb Right
Royal of his fancy, the poet himself will, even in
this present phase of his Art, " come to his Power "
and express its utmost glory in a narrative that
shall make even *Dauber* seem not " worth while,"
and *Reynard* " a dream " and *The Everlasting Mercy*
" nothing to this " ; or that, yet more greatly, he
may enter the awe and astonishment of a seventh
heaven of new inspiration, which eye hath not seen
nor ear heard nor heart conceived.

The main source of doubt is less subtle than Mr.
Murry's sensitive perception suggests to him, and lies
in the fatal fluency of the poet ; in his dangerous
over-production (though we do rush to the nearest
city on the very day of a new poem's appearance
and hunger for the day till it comes) ; in his tendency
to hurry what cannot be hurried—with the result
that even some of his best writing is patched with
crudity, " vulgarity " and appalling prosing, and
marred by needless carelessness. That he is capable
of original and lofty work without such flaws in
both prose and verse should now be evident. But
it is rather staggering and fruitful of misgiving—
though one says this with a sense of self-denial—
to find two or three books being published in a year.

Not so speedily are immortal words fashioned and
rung. It is not Mr. Masefield, but some American
versemakers of whom Mr. Murry writes that to
rush at poetry thus is to make the Muse stammer
and say what she neither wishes nor means to say.
It is to make her utter commonplace where truth
requires subtlety and fantasy and imagination.
It is an ill thing when a poet cannot wait and take
months to a single sonnet, if he must; and certainly
Mr. Masefield must needs love the ideal and the
pangs of *Adam's Curse* above aught to be gained
by following any line of less resistance, even if it
be in defiance rather than carelessness.

> A line will take us hours may be ;
> Yet if it does not seem a moment's thought,
> Our stitching and unstitching has been naught.
> Better go down upon your marrow bones
> And scrub a kitchen pavement, or break stones
> Like an old pauper, in all kinds of weather ;
> For to articulate sweet sounds together
> Is to work harder than all these, and yet
> Be thought an idler by the noisy set
> Of bankers, schoolmasters, and clergymen
> The martyrs call the world.[1]

It is disaster and the end of all things if it has to be
a race with time, and if every little space of days
must see another page dashed off, another book
rushed out.

But this is a suspected tendency rather than a
detected vice in the poet whose work I have sought
to commend and to criticise in these pages, and the
note on which I least of all should wish to end is
the note of complaint, however backed by appreciation and expectancy. With millions more I have

[1] W. B. Yeats : *Poems*, 1899-1905, p. 170.

delighted in Mr. Masefield's work, and in this essay —put together from recollections of many conversations about his poems and of little talks given among very humble students of poetry (in which, as will be seen, I have used the critical work of greater writers than myself freely and perhaps with too little acknowledgement)—I have sought to justify that delight.

BIBLIOGRAPHY

1902 Salt Water Ballads. (Elkin Mathews.)
1903 Ballads. (Elkin Mathews.)
1905 A Mainsail Haul. (Elkin Mathews.)
      Sea Life in Nelson's Time. (Methuen.)
1906 On the Spanish Main. (Methuen.)
1907 A Tarpaulin Muster. (Grant Richards.)
1908 Captain Margaret. (Grant Richards.)
1909 Multitude and Solitude. (Grant Richards.)
      The Tragedy of Nan. The Campden Wonder. Mrs. Harrison. (Grant Richards.)
1910 Lost Endeavour. (Nelson.)
      Ballads and Poems. (Elkin Mathews.)
      The Tragedy of Pompey the Great. (Sidgwick & Jackson.)
      Martin Hyde, the Duke's Messenger. (Wells Gardner, Darton.)
      My Faith in Woman Suffrage. (Woman's Press.)
      A Book of Discoveries. (Wells Gardner, Darton.)
1911 Jim Davis. (Wells Gardner, Darton.)
      The Street of To-day. (Dent.)
      The Everlasting Mercy. (Sidgwick & Jackson.)
      Shakespeare. (Williams & Norgate.)
1912 The Widow in the Bye Street. (Sidgwick & Jackson.)
1913 Dauber. (Heinemann.)
      The Daffodil Fields. (Heinemann.)
      Additions to a Mainsail Haul. (Elkin Mathews.)
1914 Philip the King and other Poems. (Heinemann.)
1915 The Faithful. (Heinemann.)
      Personal Recollections of J. M. Synge. (Cuala Press.)
1916 Good Friday. (Heinemann.)
      Sonnets and Poems (included in Lollingdon Downs). (Garden City Press.)
      The Locked Chest. The Sweeps of Ninety-Eight. (Both written ten years earlier.) (Garden City Press.)
      Gallipoli. (Heinemann.)

1917   The Old Front Line. (Heinemann.)
       Lollingdon Downs and other Poems, with Sonnets
          (Heinemann.)
1918   A Poem and Two Plays. (Heinemann.)
          (Rosas—The Locked Chest—The Sweeps of
          Ninety-Eight.)
1919   St. George and the Dragon. (Heinemann.)
       The Battle of the Somme. (Heinemann.)
       Reynard the Fox. (Heinemann.)
1920   Enslaved and other Poems, with Sonnets. (Heinemann.)
       Right Royal. (Heinemann.)
1921   King Cole. (Heinemann.)

Introductory and Editorial Works, etc. :

       A Voyage Round the World in the Years 1740–4.
          (Lord Anson)
       The Principal Navigators. (Hakluyt.)
       Travels of Marco Polo.
       Chronicles of the Pilgrim Fathers. (Morton.)
       Daughters of Ishmael. (R. W. Kauffman.)
       Poems of Keats.
       Attack. (E. G. D. Liveing.)
       The Third Miss Symons. (F. M. Mayor.)
       Poems. (R. C. Phillimore.)
       The Fancy, by " Peter Corcoran." (J. H. Reynolds.)
       Life of Nelson. (Southey.)
       Buccaneer Ballads. (E. H. Visiak.)
       Public School Verse (1919–20). Anthology.
       Dampier's Voyages.
       Selections from Defoe.
       Ruskin the Prophet. (J. H. Whitehouse.)
       Poems of Herrick.
       Doctor Faustus. (Marlowe.)
       English Prose Miscellany.
       Lyrics of Ben Jonson, Beaumont and Fletcher.
       A Sailor's Garland.
       Essays Moral and Polite, 1660–1714 (with Constance
          Masefield).
       Lyrics of the Restoration (with Constance Masefield).

Among many recent articles on Mr. Masefield's work, the following may be instanced :

John Masefield : by Arnold Bennett. (*New Age,* April 20, 1911. Reprinted in *Books and Persons,* 1917.)

The Yellow Patch : a Chronicle of Mr. John Masefield : by Dixon Scott. (*Poetry and Drama,* December 1913. Reprinted in *Men of Letters,* 1916.)

On John Masefield and the Twentieth Century Renaissance : by Charles H. Sorley. (1912. Printed in *The Letters of Charles Sorley,* 1919.)

Mr. Masefield's Secret : by Robert Lynd. (Reprinted in *Old and New Masters,* 1919.)

The Nostalgia of Mr. Masefield : by J. Middleton Murry. (*Athenæum,* January 1920. Reprinted in *Aspects of Literature,* 1920.)

Dramatists of To-Day : *III. John Masefield* : by Edward Storer. (*British Review,* December 1913.)

Some Contemporary Poets, 1920 : by Harold Monro, pp. 51–60.

Modern Dramas in Europe : by Storm Jameson, pp. 186–190.

Mr. Masefield : *Some Characteristics* : by Edward Shanks. (*London Mercury,* September 1920.)

Mr. Masefield's Fox-hunting : by Flora M. Broad. (*Poetry Review,* September–October 1920.)

The Advance of English Poetry in the Twentieth Century : by William Lyon Phelps. (Allen & Unwin, 1918.) Chapter III.

103308

DATE DUE

821.91
M396H
1969
  Hamilton, William Hamilton
   John Masefield...

Ohio Dominican College Library
1216 Sunbury Road
Columbus, Ohio 43219

DEMCO